Teachers' Rights, Duties and Responsibilities

CRONER

Croner.CCH Group Limited
145 London Road
Kingston upon Thames
Surrey KT2 6SR
Tel: 020 8547 3333

Published by
Croner.CCH Group Limited
145 London Road
Kingston upon Thames
Surrey KT2 6SR
Tel: 020 8547 3333

First published September 1997
Second Edition 1998
Third Edition 1999
Fourth Edition 2000
Fifth Edition 2001
Sixth Edition 2002

British Library cataloguing in Publication Data. A CIP Catalogue Record for this book is available from the British Library

ISBN 1 85524 666 X

Printed by Thomson Litho, Glasgow

CONTRIBUTORS

THE AUTHOR

CHRIS LOWE

The author was Head of Prince William's School, Oundle from 1971–1999. He holds degrees in English from Cambridge University and Law from London University. He has been awarded an Honorary Doctorate of Education from De Montfort University and has been Visiting Professor of Education Law at the Edith Cowan University, Perth, Western Australia. He is also an Honorary Fellow of the University of Wolverhampton and the University College of Northampton.

He has been the Honorary Legal Consultant to the Secondary Heads Association and in 1990–91 was President of SHA. He then became President of the European Secondary Heads Association (ESHA) for four years and was one of the founding members of the worldwide International Confederation of Principals.

Chris has written extensively on education management and education law, including for Croner's *Head's Legal Guide*, *Teacher's Legal Guide*, and *School Governor's Manual*. He is General Editor of both the *Teacher's Legal Guide*, and *School Governor's Manual*. He writes the weekly *Legal Issues* column in the *Times Educational Supplement*.

In 1992, he was awarded the CBE for his services to education.

THE REVIEWER

HOWARD GREEN

The reviewer was Head of the Henry Box School, Witney, Oxfordshire (1983–90) and Principal of Eggbuckland Community College, Plymouth (1992–98). He holds a degree in Natural Sciences from Cambridge University and has undertaken educational research at both Cambridge and Oxford Universities.

He set up the National Educational Assessment Centre based at Oxford Brookes University (1990–92) and, while working at the Teacher Training Agency in London, was responsible for the implementation of the Leadership Programme for Serving Headteachers. He has been a special adviser at the Department for Education and Employment and is currently an adviser to the National College for School Leadership. Howard has published widely on educational issues and is the Editorial Co-ordinator for Croner's *School Leadership* magazine.

Contents

The Curriculum

INTRODUCTION TO THE SIXTH EDITION

All teachers are affected by legislation covering the whole range of activities they are involved in. This book provides teachers with information on the laws, regulations and authoritative guidance which regulate the profession and define teachers' rights, duties and responsibilities.

The Sixth Edition has been thoroughly revised and updated, taking into account the developments in performance management and movement up the Upper Pay Spine, the new regulations regarding fixed term employment, and the provisions of the **Education Act 2002** and the **Employment Act 2002**. Some recent cases regarding teacher stress and negligence on educational visits have also been included.

The book is divided into five sections. The first section provides some background information on the structure and organisation of the education system. Sections 2 and 3 deal with teachers' conditions of service and pay and sections 4 and 5 contain information on the job of the teacher and the curriculum.

Throughout the book questions often asked by teachers are discussed and answered, with illustrations from cases which have reached the courts where relevant.

CHAPTER 1

BACKGROUND

MANAGEMENT BODIES AND AGENCIES

The Department for Education and Skills

The Department for Education and Skills (DfES) is the Government department currently overseeing the education service in England. Education in Wales is controlled by a committee reporting to the Assembly in Wales and has its own Ministers.

The DfES is led by the Secretary of State for Education and Skills with separate Ministers of State for School Standards, and Lifelong Learning and Higher Education. There are also Parliamentary Under Secretaries of State for Early Years and School Standards, Young People and Learning, and Adult Skills.

The civil servant head of department is known as the Permanent Secretary. Under the Permanent Secretary is the Secretary of State's Private Office and the Strategy and Innovation Unit, comprising a number of directorates as follows:

- Strategy and Communications
- Schools
- Youth
- Lifelong Learning
- Corporate Services and Development
- Finance and Analytical Services.

Within the Schools' Directorate there is the Standards and Effectiveness Unit, which has a particular brief for school improvement.

The Secretary of State is expected to exercise his or her powers to improve standards, encourage diversity and increase opportunities for choice in primary, secondary, further and higher education.

The Secretary of State also has the power to determine the pay and conditions of service for teachers. He or she is also empowered to have the final decision in resolving disputes and can, for example, give directions to a Local Education Authority (LEA) or board of governors that they have acted unreasonably (**Education Act 1996**, s.496).

Government Documents

The DfES periodically publishes:

(a) Reports — these usually follow a committee of enquiry and set out the findings of the committee and any recommendations the committee makes.

(b) Green Papers — consultative documents on issues which may eventually be turned into white papers.

(c) White Papers — further proposals following the initial consultation, setting out the government's policy intentions and likely legislation or regulation.

(d) Bills and Acts — a Bill is the first step towards an Act. They are set out in legislative form and are debated and voted upon by Parliament. Once the Bill has passed through Parliament and been given the Royal Assent it becomes an Act of Parliament.

(e) Statutory Instruments — these come out in the form of regulations or orders and give the detail of the implementation of the main Act. Once "laid before Parliament" they have the force of law.

(f) Guidance — used to be called "Circulars". These contain explanation of the law and regulations, and also guidance on other issues, eg anti-bullying. Some of the guidance is statutory and some non-statutory. Although non-statutory guidance does not carry the force of law, the courts would expect the guidance to be followed unless there were clear and acceptable reasons for not doing so.

(g) Codes of Practice — there are a growing number of these. They bring together advice and guidance on the practical workings of the legislation. Once again, although they are not in themselves law, those to whom they apply must "have regard" to them and they may be used in court as evidence if a person is alleged to have broken the law.

(h) Local Government Ombudsman Reports — Members of the public (usually parents in education cases) may complain to the Commission for Local Administration (the Ombudsman) about alleged maladministration by local authorities and schools. The Ombudsman will investigate and make recommendations where necessary. Reports of the investigations are made public.

The National Assembly for Wales — Education and Lifelong Learning Committee

The Committee's remit is based on the portfolio of the Minister for Education and Lifelong Learning. The Minister's portfolio embraces education and lifelong learning, which includes amongst other things the national curriculum and qualifications, all aspects of schools administration and organisation, further and higher education, supply side employment policy, including the New Deal and the work of the employment service, career services and work related training.

There is an overlapping interest with the Health and Social Services Committee which has responsibility for children and young people.

General Teaching Council

The **Teaching and Higher Education Act 1998** established a General Teaching Council (GTC)for England as a corporate body. Its principal aims are to contribute to improving the standards of teaching and the quality of learning and to maintain and improve standards of professional conduct amongst teachers. There are separate arrangements for the GTC in Wales.

The Council advises the Secretary of State on matters referred to it, particularly on the role of the teaching profession, and the standards of teaching and conduct of teachers, and their career development, training and performance management, recruitment and medical fitness to teach.

The Council will keep a register of teachers and will issue a code laying down the standards of professional conduct and practice expected of teachers. Members will pay fees to the Council in order to ensure that the body has sufficient funding to be able to speak out for members, most of whom are teachers.

The Council also has disciplinary powers under which regulations will provide for it to take action in cases of allegations of unacceptable professional conduct, or serious incompetence, or where a teacher has been convicted of a relevant offence.

Professional Code

The Council has issued a Code of Practice defining the beliefs, values and attitudes that underlie the teaching profession. Its main aim is to affirm the high standards of teacher professionalism and to provide guidance for those in the profession.

National College for School Leadership

The National College for School Leadership (NCSL) exists to improve the quality of school leadership, and consequently student achievement. It runs training programmes and initiates research programmes. The NCSL has responsibility for the three national programmes for headship:

- the National Professional Qualification for Headship (NPQH)
- Headlamp (the induction programme)
- the Leadership Programme for Serving Headteachers (LPSH).

The Teacher Training Agency

The Teacher Training Agency (TTA) advises the Secretary of State on matters covering the recruitment and training of teachers. It accredits providers of initial training of teachers and other in-service training.

Local Education Authority

Local Education Authorities (LEAs) are democratically elected local councils which have responsibility for providing education in their areas.

One of their prime functions is to determine the amount of money that should be spent on schools and the formula for delegating the budget to each school.

Under the provisions of the **School Standards and Framework Act 1998** (SSFA), LEAs have the additional duty to promote high standards in primary and secondary schools, for those being educated otherwise than at a school and for all registered pupils.

Every LEA must have a School Organisation Plan setting out how it proposes to provide primary and secondary education to meet the needs of the population of its area and an Education Development Plan containing the LEA's proposals to demonstrate how it intends to raise the standards of education in its schools and improve their performance.

Each LEA must establish a School Organisation Committee in accordance with regulations the Secretary of State will publish. Once set up, the committee will be independent of the LEA. Other than this requirement, LEAs are free to organise themselves as they wish. They are not obliged to appoint an Education Committee, but most do so.

The council will be advised by a Chief Education Officer (CEO) although they are often given different titles. The CEO is the council's chief executive officer for education and has various rights and duties *vis a vis* schools.

LEA and Schools Partnerships

A Code of Practice on LEA-school relations has established the principle that schools and LEAs should work together to achieve higher standards. The general assumption is, however, that the balance in the partnership is tipped towards the autonomy of the school.

Any intervention by the LEA should normally be at the invitation of the school and, where an LEA uses its residual powers of intervention, it should not come as a surprise to the school.

Governing Bodies

Governing bodies of maintained schools are made up of representatives of local authorities, churches, business, parents, school staff and the community, depending on the nature of the school. Governing bodies of maintained schools have the responsibility for the conduct and direction of the school and have a duty to promote high standards of educational achievement at the school.

Governing bodies, even of LEA maintained schools, have wide powers and duties, particularly in the areas of employment, health and safety, the curriculum and school funds.

Following the **Education Act 2002** schools may now operate under a single governing body if they choose. Governing bodies will become more autonomous, with more control over some aspects of teachers' pay and conditions and the National Curriculum.

The criteria for defining a successful school will be set out in future regulations.

Governing bodies will be able to form companies in order to provide services for schools, and to exercise some LEA functions. There will be pilot projects to discover what works best.

It is usual for independent schools as well as maintained schools to have governing bodies but some independent schools are limited companies or have a sole proprietor.

Financial Delegation of School Budgets

The **Education Reform Act 1988** (now consolidated in the **Education Act 1996**) required LEAs to delegate the management of budgets to their schools. An increasing share of the LEAs budget is now passed to the school. The governors usually delegate the actual management of the budget to the Head, while retaining the overview and responsibility.

As well as financial management, some staffing issues are also delegated — complement of staff, appointments, dismissals and discipline, for example. Local schemes of management of schools vary in their details.

Education Action Zones

Education Action Zones (EAZs) have been set up under the **School Standards and Framework Act 1998** to improve the standards in the provision of education at particular maintained schools. Each EAZs has between 15 and 25 secondary and primary schools, and is managed by a Forum of partners. The Forum also administers the funding from the DfES and private funds. The EAZs is not controlled by an LEA, but each school is part of its LEA for other than EAZs purposes.

In addition, there are Small Education Action Zones (SEAZs) which comprise a number of primary schools and one secondary school.

In 2004 the EAZs will be phased out and be replaced by other groupings based on the best practice learned through the EAZ project and other government initiatives.

New Opportunities Fund

The funding for this comes from the National Lottery. It can be used for any purpose designated by the Government. Much of the enhancement of Information and Communications Technology (ICT) and ICT training has come from this fund. In 2001 it was announced that over £205 million is available to create and develop regular out-of-school-hours learning activities involving half of all secondary schools and special schools, and a quarter of all primary schools around the school day, weekends and in the holidays.

The Fund will also be providing finance for a Green Spaces and Sustainable Communities programme, which will aim to transform children's play areas and upgrade green spaces in local communities.

The Qualifications and Curriculum Authority

The Qualifications and Curriculum Authority (QCA) was set up in the **Education Act 1997**. Its functions are set out in ss.22–24. The main aim of the QCA is to promote coherence and improve attainment in education and training. It works closely with awarding bodies, national training organisations, education bodies, employers and other key players. With respect to maintained schools it has duties to review all matters concerned with the curriculum and school examinations and assessment. It advises the Secretary of State on these matters.

The comparable body in Wales is Awdurdod Cymwysterau, Cwricwlwm ac Asesu Cymru.

The British Educational Communications and Technology Agency

The British Educational Communications and Technology Agency (BECTA) took over the work of the National Council for Educational Technology in 1998. It advises the Secretary of State on matters concerned with the development of ICT in schools.

The Technology Trust

The Technology Trust is a non-government organisation which raises financial support for the development of technology and for specialist colleges of all types. It also advises the Government on educational technology issues. Schools can become affiliated to the Trust on payment of a fee, for which they receive access to training literature, advice and sponsorship.

School Teachers' Review Body

The School Teachers' Review Body (STRB) makes recommendations to the Secretary of State on the pay and conditions of employment for teachers in England and Wales. Recommendations that the Secretary of State accepts have statutory force.

Office for Standards in Education

The Office for Standards in Education (OFSTED) is a Government department headed by Her Majesty's Chief Inspector for Schools (HMCI). A similar post exists for Wales.

HMCI has a duty to keep the Secretary of State informed about standards in schools and to organise regular inspections of schools.

In addition to reporting on the quality of teaching in national curriculum subjects and religious education, the inspectors are obliged to report on equal opportunity and special educational needs issues.

The reports must also state the percentage of teaching which was:

- very good or better
- satisfactory or better
- less than satisfactory.

The inspectors also grade each lesson that they observe. There are three levels — excellent/very good, good/satisfactory and unsatisfactory/poor.

Her Majesty's Inspectors (HMIs) are also appointed for particular posts of responsibility.

OFSTED organises regular inspections of schools. For this purpose trained Registered Inspectors (RIs) are appointed to form inspection teams. They are private teams but responsible to HMCI for the conduct of the inspection and the inspection report. The RI is required to ensure that the team for each inspection contains at least one *lay inspector,* ie someone without personal experience of managing or teaching in a school. They may, however, have been a governor or voluntary helper in a school. RIs have to submit tenders for each inspection.

New inspection arrangements

From 2000, schools have been inspected in accordance with the provisions of the revised OFSTED framework, "Inspecting Schools". The new framework incorporates all the major changes in policy, including: short inspections, principle of "best value", performance management, reduction in notice period (now fixed at between six and ten weeks), and greater emphasis on educational inclusion.

The School Teachers' Pay and Conditions Document

The *School Teachers' Pay and Conditions Document* (the Blue Book or Document) is published annually and sets out statutory provisions relating to the employment of teachers in England and Wales. (The provisions are dealt with in the sections on *Teachers' Conditions of Service, Teachers' Pay* and *The Teacher's Job*).

The Burgundy Book

The *Conditions of Service of School Teachers in England and Wales* (referred to as the *Burgundy Book* because of its colour) contains agreements between employers' representatives and teacher unions. It preceded the *School Teachers' Pay and Conditions of Service Document* (The Blue Book), but still contains agreements that will form part of teachers' contracts such as maternity leave arrangements, grievance procedures, sick pay, etc.

LEAs and school governing bodies will either have adopted these agreements or replaced them with locally negotiated agreements.

The *Burgundy Book* is, therefore, largely redundant.

The Connexions Service

The service provides information, advice and guidance for all young people aged between 13 and 19, to help them make the most of their educational and vocational opportunities. One of the main aims is to prepare young people for successful transition to work and adult responsibilities; future plans include the provision of personal advisors for individuals.

DEFINITION OF A PARENT

The definition of a parent includes actual parents, anyone who is not a parent but has parental responsibility and someone who has care of a child.

All of these are entitled to receive information about the school and the pupil — subject to any court order to the contrary (see the **Children Act 1989**).

TYPES OF SCHOOL

A school is defined in the **Education Act 1997** as:

> "an education institution which is outside the further and higher education sectors, and which provides primary or secondary education or both. It is a school even if it provides part-time education suitable to the requirements of junior pupils or further education."

It is the parents' duty to send children of compulsory school age to school or to arrange efficient full-time education for them elsewhere.

Independent Schools

Independent schools are not maintained by Government or by LEAs but have to be registered with the DfES. Some are commercial employers, others are non-profit-making charities.

The former Assisted Places scheme, through which certain pupils' fees for attending independent schools were paid, is in the process of being phased out.

Diversity of Schools

The new Education Act presages the creation of a more diverse system of secondary education with every school having its own individual ethos, mission and character. The plans include the creation of a new designation of Advanced Specialist School open to high performing schools (after demonstrating success as part of the Specialist school programme) and the expansion of the City Academy programme (see below).

Specialist Colleges

A growing number of secondary schools are becoming "specialist colleges". The schools have to obtain cash sponsorship from private partners, and if accepted into the programme, they also receive capital and revenue funding from the DfES. The existing categories of specialism are:

- technology
- languages
- performing arts
- sport.

From September 2002, there have been additional new categories:

- business and enterprise
- science
- engineering
- mathematics and computing.

City Academies

City Academies are maintained secondary schools in cities, which obtain private capital and revenue sponsorship in order to become one. They will then be independent of LEA control and will receive direct funding from the DfES. The first City Academies are due to open from 2001 onwards — they are being established on a similar basis to existing

City Technology Colleges (CTCs). The new **Education Bill 2001** envisages an expansion of the programme to facilitate the addition of more faith schools and schools for 5–18 year olds.

Beacon Schools

Schools which have exceptional OFSTED reports can be invited by the Secretary of State to become "Beacon Schools", though there is no obligation to do so. Beacon schools receive extra government money to enable them to help less successful schools.

Training Schools

Schools which have a strong reputation for initial teacher training and continuing professional development. They are recognised by the DfES and receive additional funding to support this work and share their good practice.

Maintained Schools

Maintained schools are those which are largely maintained by the local authority. They are divided into the following categories:

- community schools
- foundation schools
- voluntary schools (voluntary aided schools and voluntary controlled schools)
- community special schools
- foundation special schools.

Voluntary aided schools

All premises costs are shared between the voluntary body, LEA, and the Secretary of State. Recurring costs are met by the LEA.

The founding body appoints foundation governors who form a majority on the governing body.

The governing body are the employers of staff, although the LEA pays them.

Voluntary controlled schools

These schools are owned by the voluntary body but costs are met by the LEA. Staff are employed by the LEA but the school has foundation governors. Under the new legislation this category will disappear and schools will choose which category they wish to join.

Community schools

Community schools were formerly called county schools. They are maintained by a local education authority, which will be responsible for funding them. The school's budget is then delegated to the governors of the school who can spend the amounts as agents of the LEA.

The control and direction of community schools are the responsibility of each governing body.

Foundation schools

These are the former grant-maintained schools. Foundation refers to the fact that a body of persons holds land or other property on behalf of the school. They now come under the maintenance of an LEA, and their governing bodies are not responsible for any of the costs of maintaining the school.

Governing Bodies

Governing bodies of maintained schools are made up of representatives of local authorities, churches, business, parents, school staff and the community, depending on the nature of the school. Governing bodies of maintained schools have the responsibility for the conduct and direction of the school and have a duty to promote high standards of educational achievement at the school. Governing bodies, even of LEA maintained schools, have wide powers and duties, particularly in the areas of employment, health and safety, the curriculum and school funds. It is usual for independent schools as well as maintained schools to have governing bodies but some independent schools are limited companies or have a sole proprietor.

How many governors do schools have ?

There are different numbers in the categories of governors for different sizes and types of school. The composition of the various governing bodies are set out in Annex A of the DfES circular 15/98 *New Framework for Governing Bodies.*

Relevant Body

This can refer to the local authority maintaining a school without a delegated budget, or to the governing body for schools with delegated budgets, or to the governing body of a foundation or voluntary school. In the case of unattached teachers, the relevant body is the body by which he or she is employed.

Raising Standards

The Government is committed to raising standards of achievement throughout the maintained system and has introduced a large number of measures to promote this aim, eg the literacy and numeracy programmes, reduction in class sizes, target setting, performance management, education action zones, Excellence in Cities partnerships, Excellence Challenge and so on. The **Education Bill 2001** envisages more initiatives, including:

- the introduction of measures to ensure that educational provision will be more closely linked to individual's talents and aspirations, particularly from the age of 14
- introducing fixed-term "standard contracts" to enable private, voluntary and faith organisations to support the management of schools
- increasing schools' autonomy and freedom to innovate
- reinforcing accountability arrangements at school and LEA levels to ensure the delivery of high standards.

TYPES OF TEACHER

Schools are required by teacher regulations to be staffed by a sufficient number of *suitable* teachers to secure the education of the pupils.

Qualified Teacher Status

Except for special arrangements relating to hearing and visually impaired pupils, all teachers must be qualified in accordance with Schedule 3 of the **Education (Teachers) Regulations 1993** (SI 1993 No. 543).

There are various ways of obtaining qualified teacher status but the most common way is an approved course for a Bachelor of Education degree or Post-Graduate Certificate in Education (PGCE). There is also a Graduate Teacher Programme (GTP) for graduates, whose first degrees and previous education provide the foundation for work as teachers in the phase (primary or secondary) and subject(s) they wish to teach. A Registered Teacher Programme (RTP) provides for non-graduates who have successfully completed the equivalent of at least two years' full-time relevant education. RTP trainees must be at least 24 years old and must hold at least grade C equivalent in English and Mathematics prior to entry.

Both programmes normally last one year but can be shorter. The minimum is three months.

After obtaining the teaching qualification, newly qualified teachers (NQTs) must complete satisfactorily a year's induction programme in a relevant school. The requirements are set out in Circular 5/99 *The Induction Period for Newly Qualified Teachers* and describes the arrangements for NQTs to complete their induction period.

It combines an individualised programme of monitoring and support with an assessment of performance. Annex A sets out the standards for determining whether or not an induction period has been completed satisfactorily.

Fast Track

The Fast Track (FT) programme was first proposed in the government's Green Paper "Teachers: meeting the challenge" in 1998. Its purpose is to attract the most able graduates into teaching and to move outstanding teachers rapidly through the profession to reach their full potential and take on leadership roles in the shortest possible time.

Existing teachers have been able to join the programme from 2001. The first Fast Track teachers were in post in 2002. Recruits from outside the profession began Initial Teacher Training in 2001.

Teachers From Outside England And Wales

Persons who have completed initial teacher training in Scotland or Northern Ireland or nationals of an EU country who have completed a course of professional teacher training of at least three years' duration can obtain Qualified Teacher Status (QTS).

Non-European Economic Area Overseas Trained Teachers

From April 2001 it has been possible for non-European Economic Area (EEA) overseas trained teachers to work in England and secure QTS status without further training. They are able to work for up to four years as temporary teachers either in one school or a number of schools before they need to secure QTSstatus in order to remain in a teaching post.

Unlike previously, there is no longer any need for them to spend three months training on the Graduate Teacher Programme before they could be assessed against QTS standards. Now there is no minimum training period, and they can present themselves for assessment without further training if they wish.

Non-EEA overseas trained teachers with at least two years' full-time (or part-time equivalent) teaching experience will also be able to present themselves for assessment against the Induction standards as well as the QTS standards, and may be granted exemption from the requirement to serve an induction year.

Part-time Teachers

Teachers may be engaged as either permanent or temporary part-time teachers. Under the **Part-time Workers (Prevention of Less Favourable Treatment) Regulations 2000**, part-time staff now have the same employment rights as full-time employees, regardless of the number of hours worked each week or the length of continuous service.

Fixed-term Contracts

Some contracts can be for a specified period and will specify an end-date. These are usually contracts covering a maternity or sickness leave, but there can be many other reasons. Such contracts will automatically terminate at the end of that period without the need for any notice to be given, or any dismissal procedures to be followed. It is possible, however, for some fixed term contracts to provide that notice can be given during the term of the contract.

The termination of a fixed term contract is still technically a dismissal in law. Therefore, if a fixed term contract is for one year or more the employee will have employment protection rights at the end of the fixed term.

The Fixed Term Employees (Prevention of Less Favourable Treatment) Regulations 2001 took effect on 1 October 2002.

The Regulations prevent employers (LEAs, governing bodies, or proprietors of independent schools) from treating employees on fixed term contracts less favourably than those on comparable "permanent" contracts, unless the employer can show an objective reason. Fixed term contracts must be equivalent to those of full-time staff in comparative posts, which means that fixed term employees must have the same access to promotion, training, performance review and other benefits enjoyed by full-time employees.

The Regulations impose restrictions on the renewal of fixed term contracts. Fixed term employees must not be treated less favourably than full-time employees as far as the length of service required in order to be entitled to contractual benefits.

The practice of adding waiver clauses to fixed term employees' contracts, which has prevented them from claiming statutory redundancy benefit at the end of a fixed term contract, has been stopped.

Unless employers and employees reach a collective agreement on a limit to the use of successive fixed term contracts, an employee who has worked under successive fixed-term contracts for four years will have permanent status.

Job Sharing

Job sharing is a form of part-time employment where two people voluntarily share the duties and responsibilities of one full-time post. It has now become a more common practice. A full-time post can be shared between one or more teachers with agreed times. Such contracts are in reality a number of individual part-time contracts. The trick is to ensure that the job descriptions, loading and pay are all agreed and that any subsequent changes are reasonable and, preferably, agreed in advance.

Such a situation demands a good deal of mutual trust and flexibility and, in most cases, job sharing works well. These contracts are particularly attractive to women returners and women with small children, even though increasingly men are being drawn into job sharing. Because of this imbalance between women and men part-time teachers, attempts to terminate these part-time contracts can lead to problems for the school.

In *Tickle v Governors of Riverview First School and Surrey C.C.* (1993), a part-timer involved in a job share with a colleague was replaced by a full-time, newly qualified teacher. It transpired that the reason was financial. An Industrial Tribunal held that Mrs Tickle had been indirectly discriminated against. The requirement to work full-time was a condition of continued employment in the school and also a condition for being considered for the new permanent post. The Tribunal considered that the proportion of female teachers who could comply with this was smaller than the number of males who could.

The governors had been unreasonable in not allowing Mrs Tickle the opportunity to make representations on the suitability of continuing with part-time employment. Also, the job was not advertised and neither job sharer was invited to apply. The governors were unable to give a good reason for replacing the job sharers with a single full-time teacher. Although the Tribunal agreed that the school needed a full-time teacher for greater security and continuity for the class, this has to be balanced against any likely discriminatory effects.

It seemed that financial rather than educational motives lay behind the move and these were seen to be unjustifiable.

Unattached Teachers

Unattached teachers are teachers who are not employed at a specific school or whose place of employment is somewhere other than a school, eg peripatetic music teachers, special needs teachers or teachers who work in a Pupil Referral Unit (PRU).

Unattached teachers have their salaries determined by the LEA in accordance with whichever provisions in the *School Teachers' Pay and Conditions Document* the LEA thinks is appropriate.

Teachers in PRUs may be paid according to the class teachers' scale or the Deputy Head or Head scales.

If they are paid as class teachers, then they are subject to the same conditions of service and working time provisions as classroom teachers in schools.

Supply Teachers

Under the conditions of the School Teachers' Pay and Conditions Document (SCPCD), LEAs and governing bodies of maintained schools are required to provide supply cover for any teacher not available to teach for a period in excess of three days, or where non-availability is known at least 48 hours in advance, for all such absences.

LEAs and schools usually keep a list of short-term supply teachers.

It is also possible for teachers to be engaged for a short or long term, during the absence of a teacher through sickness or on maternity leave or secondment, or other reasons. In such cases, as in all fixed-term contracts, the date or the specific event, eg "the return of the absent teacher", should be clear in the contract.

Short-notice teachers (supply teachers) are usually paid on a daily basis calculated as a fraction of 195 days (the traditional teachers' year — see page 34).

Although the Pay and Conditions Document does not specify a length of the working day, it is recommended by the DfES that this should be considered as 6.5 hours of working time, including time set aside for required duties other than teaching pupils. Such teachers should be offered the opportunity of being involved in other duties and should then be paid the full rate. Where they cannot be available for work beyond the pupil day, the pay calculation is *pro rata*.

Supply cover teachers who are covering for a term or less are covered by all of the conditions of service contained in the Burgundy Book except for:

- the arrangements related to notice
- the procedures relating to dismissal unless on the grounds of capability
- maternity leave provisions.

Those engaged on an hourly rate are not covered by the following exceptions:

- grievance procedures
- compensation for assaults and losses
- travelling expenses
- suspension or termination on medical grounds
- leave for public duties, moderation or personal circumstances
- provisions relating to holidays and the working day
- disciplinary procedures.

Tax and National Insurance

Supply teachers employed by an LEA or school are subject to tax and national insurance (NI) arrangements under LEA or school Pay As You Earn (PAYE).

If the teacher is employed by an agency, the agency is responsible.

Self-employed teachers are responsible for making their own arrangements.

How do I know whether I am being paid the right daily rate as a short-notice teacher?

If a short-notice teacher is a qualified teacher the relevant body must formally assess his or her total of points in the same way as for a full-time teacher.

Although technically this means that a new calculation should be made for every new appointment, in practice a point assessment is made at the first appointment in a new school year and a record kept by the school, LEA and the teacher. This cuts out possible delays in getting salaries paid.

Unqualified short-notice teachers are paid in accordance with the pay scale for unqualified teachers (see below).

Short notice teachers may also be given full or half points for responsibilities, excellence or special needs in the same way as a full-time teacher. This rarely happens however, and only the points for qualifications and experience are carried forward to the next appointment.

For more details of the points system, see *Chapter 3, Teachers' Pay.*

Use Of Supply Teachers

Supply teachers are teachers who are not on the school's permanent staff but are brought in to cover vacancies, usually on a daily basis.

Circular 7/96 *Use of Supply Teachers* gives guidance on the employment position of supply teachers.

Supply teachers at maintained schools are covered by the normal appointment requirements of the **Education Reform Act 1988** (now consolidated in the **School Standards and Framework Act 1998**), except in circumstances where the supply teacher is covering for a temporary absence and is not, therefore, filling a vacancy or where he or she is self-employed or employed by an agency.

A vacant post can also be filled temporarily for up to four months.

Checks

Before employing a supply teacher, a school will check:

- identity
- permission to work
- qualifications
- health
- previous employment history
- records of barred teachers

• criminal records.

In order to check the criminal record of an applicant a school has to ask the applicant to apply to the Criminal Records Bureau for a "Declaration". Only the applicant can do this, and only the registered agency (usually the LEA for community schools, and the school itself in the case of foundation, aided and independent schools) and the applicant can receive the Declaration.

Supply teachers should normally have Qualified Teacher Status (QTS). A supply teacher employed to teach sensory impaired children must also have (or intend to have within three years) a relevant qualification. Some exceptions are possible, eg a person holding authorisation under the Licensed Overseas Trained Teacher Schemes.

Maintained schools must ensure that supply teachers have the health and physical capacity for the job.

Checking with the GTC

All teachers working in maintained and non-maintained special schools and Pupil Referral Units in England must register with the GTC, unless they are exempt from having to hold QT status.

Employers must check with the GTC whether applicants are registered with the Council and whether any restrictions on their employment are in force.

Agency Teachers

The employment status of supply teachers depends on the circumstances.

Supply teachers recruited through an agency are not employed directly by the LEA or school governing body following a court decision in *TimePlan Education Group v National Union of Teachers and Another* (1995). A consequence of this is that such teachers are not subject to the provisions of the School Teachers' Pay and Conditions legislation.

However, governing bodies and Heads have the power to direct reasonably the agency teacher as to the work to be undertaken in their school.

Supply teachers employed by an agency will receive a daily rate of pay agreed with the agency. This will be lower than the rate paid directly by the school or LEA.

Unqualified Teachers

Can I teach in a school without any formal qualifications?

Schools are permitted to employ instructors to teach any art, skill or subject requiring special qualifications or experience for which no qualified teacher is available. An instructor does not have general teaching responsibilities but in all other respects has a responsibility for the oversight and control of pupils in the specialist area.

Barred Teachers

It is unlawful for a school to employ any teacher who has been barred by the Secretary of State (see *Chapter 2, Teachers' Conditions of Service*). This also applies to independent schools.

Permission to Work in the UK

Foreign nationals must have permission to work in this country. Nationals of Gibraltar and of countries in the European Economic Area (EEA) do not need permission and are employable on the same basis as UK nationals.

Work permits are only issued for specific jobs. The Overseas Labour Service at the Department for Education and Skills (DfES), 45 Moorfoot, Sheffield S1 4PQ can give further advice.

New arrangements for non-EEA teachers are set out on page 16.

Can I, as a Commonwealth national, teach in a UK school?

Commonwealth nationals admitted to the UK as working holidaymakers are permitted to finance their stay by casual work without a permit. They could, therefore, work as a supply teacher on a part-time basis for most of their holiday or full-time for up to half their holiday (maximum one year). They will not be permitted to continue working in the UK after the expiry of their visa. Note the changes to the arrangements for non-EEA teachers set out on page 16.

The Human Rights Act 1998

The **Human Rights Act 1998** provides for certain human rights issues, which previously had to be argued in the European Human Rights Court, to be taken to British courts. Human rights are, of course, a major issue for teachers as well as others, but since most British legislation has already taken into account the European human rights directives, no great rush to the courts is expected.

CHAPTER 2

TEACHERS' CONDITIONS OF SERVICE

BECOMING A TEACHER

Governing bodies of maintained schools are responsible for appointing teaching and non-teaching staff to the school, although they can expect advice from LEAs. Where maintained schools are not in financial delegation schemes, the LEA assumes overall control of the appointment procedures, although the sifting and interviewing is likely to be largely in the hands of the governing body and the Head.

The prescribed procedure is set out in Schedules 16 and 17 of the **Schools Standards and Framework Act 1998**. It applies to full-time and part-time posts. It does not apply to temporary appointments of less than four months pending the return to work of the holder or a permanent appointment.

The procedure is as follows.

1. The governors must determine a specification for the post in consultation with the Head. This will normally form the basis of an advertisement and job description. A copy of this must be sent to the LEA.
2. The governing body must then advertise the post, unless it makes an internal appointment or accepts a suitably qualified teacher nominated by the LEA. This teacher must be an employee of the LEA, or be about to take up employment at a future date with the LEA, or be employed by a governing body of an aided school maintained by the LEA.

3. An advertisement must be in a manner likely to come to the notice of appropriate candidates.
4. When a post has been advertised the governors must interview candidates they consider suitable, including any LEA nominated persons.
5. Finally, the governors recommend to the LEA a person to be appointed.
6. The governing body can delegate the responsibility for selecting staff (other than a Head or deputy head) to the Head alone and/or one or more governors. Even if the Head is not part of the selection panel, he or she has a right to be present and to offer advice on the appointment. It is rare these days for representatives of the Chief Education Officer to be present at interviews for assistant teachers, but it is possible. If present, they have a right to offer advice to the selection panel.
7. If governors cannot agree on a suitable appointment they can repeat the steps without necessarily re-advertising.
8. The LEA must appoint the person recommended unless he or she does not meet relevant "staff qualifications" which are defined in Schedule 3 as qualifications, health and physical capacity and fitness on educational grounds or on any other respect which for the time being apply under regulations barring people for misconduct.

Application Forms

It is usual for application forms to be provided with a request to add supplementary information in a letter or curriculum vitae.

Can I leave out details of serious illness or a careless driving conviction?

A failure to disclose material facts will lead to the withdrawal of the offer of appointment or dismissal if the appointment has been confirmed. It is even possible to be prosecuted for attempting to obtain monies by fraudulent means.

Giving inaccurate medical information can also lead to dismissal. The decision to dismiss a teacher who had given false information has been upheld in the courts and many dismissals on this ground have actually taken place.

Under the **Access to Medical Reports Act 1988**, schools and LEAs can request an applicant to consent to his or her doctor being approached for a medical report.

Am I protected by the Rehabilitation of Offenders Act 1974?

Teaching posts are one of the categories exempt from the provisions of the Act (see below).

Applicants will have to declare any convictions, cautions or bind-overs which they have incurred, including any that might be considered "spent" under the Rehabilitation of Offenders Act. If you are appointed to a post you will be asked to apply to the Criminal Records Bureau for a "Disclosure" to verify your declaration.

References

Does the Head have to provide a reference for me when I apply for a new post?

The Conditions of Employment of Headteachers places an obligation on Heads to provide information about the work and performance of staff where this is relevant to their future employment.

Former employees as well as current employees have a right to expect a reference.

How can I be sure that the Head has told the truth about me in a reference?

Many references are still confidential but, increasingly, open references are being used and both you and the prospective employer will know precisely what is written. Often the Head will discuss the reference with a teacher before finalising it.

The employer (or Head) is responsible for ensuring that he or she has exercised reasonable care and skill in writing the reference and must also ensure that nothing in it can be construed as defamation. This is not the same as being honest and frank, which are part of the Head's duty to the receiving school. It is possible for a candidate for a post to see his or her reference at the receiving school, because of the provisions of the Data Protection legislation.

Appointment

After a recommendation has been made to the LEA, the LEA should investigate references, check List 99 and enquire into criminal or medical backgrounds.

The LEA (or clerk to governors of aided schools) will then write to the candidate confirming the offer of appointment. The candidate has 14 days to accept in writing.

Within eight weeks of taking up the employment, the employer must give the employee a written statement which will:

- identify the parties
- specify the date when employment began
- specify the date when the period of continuous employment began (taking into account any employment with a previous employer which counts towards that period).

The statement must also contain details of remuneration and payment periods, conditions of employment, holidays, pension schemes, place of work, disciplinary rules, grievance procedures and other matters (see page 31).

Job Descriptions

A newly appointed teacher will receive a job description around the same time as their letter of appointment. It may be fairly short, giving a job title and referring to statutory duties and a general job description, or it may be a detailed list of tasks.

Nevertheless, a teacher can be called upon by the Head or LEA to do other tasks not contained in the job description, so long as they are reasonable, necessary in the circumstances and the employee is not being treated more unfavourably than other teachers.

The High Court in *Sim v Rotherham M.B.C* (1986) held that teachers were members of a profession where obligations were not confined to imparting academic knowledge. Each teacher has a duty to co-operate in the running of the school, according to directions given by the Head. Since then the major categories of teachers' conditions of employment are laid down in the annual *School Teachers' Pay and Conditions Document*.

Medical Fitness

A teacher at a maintained school cannot be appointed to or remain at a school unless the employer is satisfied as to his or her health and physical capacity. The Secretary of State also has the power to require a medical report and to bar a teacher from employment if the report is unsatisfactory (**Education (Teachers) (Amendment) (No. 2) Regulations 1995** (SI 1995 No. 2594)). The responsibility for determining medical fitness rests with the employer.

Can a teacher be sacked for HIV or AIDS?

HIV and AIDS should be treated in exactly the same way as other illnesses. Any sudden dismissal is likely to be unlawful. There are rules covering sick leave and sick pay and only when concern for the individual teacher and his or her classes reaches the same point as for other cases of long-term illness should the school authorities be considering the possibility of dismissal on the ground of ill-health.

Physical and Mental Fitness to Teach

Circular 4/99 *Physical and Mental Fitness to Teach of Teachers* gives guidance on the procedures for assessing the physical and mental fitness to teach of those intending to become teachers and existing teachers.

No teacher can be appointed to teach unless the employers are satisfied that the employee has the necessary health and physical capacity.

The circular carefully points out that disabled people can be medically fit to teach, though employers may have to make reasonable adjustments under the **Disability Discrimination Act 1995** in order to enable disabled teachers to carry out their duties effectively.

Disabled Teachers

Circular 3/97 *What the Disability Discrimination Act 1995 means for Schools and LEAs* defines disability. It should be read alongside the guide *Employing Disabled People — A Good Practice Guide for Managers and Employers*. It is contained in a pack of cards summarising the guide's advice.

Interviews

Most appointments of teaching staff are made after an interview. The panel may consist statutorily of the Head or one or more governors, or a combination of Head and governors. It is usual for an appropriate line manager (eg head of department) to be involved too.

The questions and procedures should ensure equity to all candidates. Discriminatory questions should not be used, nor questions about trade union membership, nor questions in respect of religious or political convictions. However, for appointments in aided schools and certain "reserved" post appointments in controlled schools and special agreement schools, governors may ask questions of a religious nature.

How should I deal with discriminatory questions?

If a discriminatory question is asked, a candidate would be right to refuse to answer. This is not always easy in an interview situation, but a polite statement to the chair of the panel that you do not wish to answer the question because it appears to be discriminatory may lead to the question being withdrawn or re-phrased. In many cases, the Head or chair will intervene to make the point for you.

Induction

All newly qualified teachers (NQTs) must complete an induction period of three school terms if they wish to work in a maintained school or non-maintained special school in England. NQTs will have to complete successfully an induction period of three terms or equivalent in a maintained school or non-maintained special school or a prescribed independent school.

The induction period will contain an individualised programme of monitoring and support, based in part on the Career Entry Profile (CEP) and including an induction tutor and an assessment of their performance.

The standards that the NQTs are expected to reach are laid down in Annex A of Circular 5/99 *The Induction Period for Newly Qualified Teachers.*

They cover:

- planning
- teaching and class management
- monitoring, assessment, recording, reporting and accountability
- the discharge of any other professional duties.

The Circular gives guidance on the monitoring and support, the assessment arrangements and the action to be taken if the NQTs is showing signs of unsatisfactory performance.

Teachers in the induction period will not be subject to the performance review (appraisal) process. They will be required to teach no more than 90% of the hours taught by substantive teachers in the school.

Redeployment

Where an LEA has two or more schools it maintains which do not have delegated budgets, it is possible for teachers to be redeployed to another school where there is a reorganisation or in the event of falling rolls.

Normally, however, it is not possible for a teacher to be redeployed without the consent of the receiving school's governing body. Some LEAs run voluntary schemes for their schools which the governing bodies opt into.

CONTRACTS AND CONDITIONS OF SERVICE

All contracts of employment are governed by employment protection legislation, which gives minimum rights to all employees. Employers are free to add to these rights in specific contracts.

All employees are entitled to receive from their employers, no later than eight weeks after the beginning of their employment, a written statement which must:

- identify the parties
- specify the date when employment began
- specify the date when the period of continuous employment began, taking into account any employment with a previous employer which counts towards continuous employment (in the case of a teacher, a move from a school in one LEA to one in another LEA would constitute continuous employment).

The statement must also contain the following terms as at a date specified which is not more than one week prior to the date on which the statement is given:

- scale of pay
- payment intervals (in the case of teachers this is usually monthly)
- conditions relating to hours of work
- holiday entitlement
- terms relating to incapacity for work, including any provision for sick pay
- pension scheme
- length of notice of termination of employment
- job title or description
- period of employment if not permanent
- place of work
- any collective agreements which affect the terms and conditions
- a note concerning any disciplinary rules or reference to a document where they can be found (this is not applicable to employers with fewer than 20 employees)
- procedures for settling grievances.

COMMON LAW DUTIES OF EMPLOYERS AND EMPLOYEES

In addition to statutory duties, employers have common law duties as follows:

- a duty to pay, even when work is not required
- a duty of care, most of which is now subscribed in health and safety legislation of a duty of reasonableness — the law expects mutual trust and unreasonable behaviour breaks this trust and will normally lead to a breach of contract.

In return, employees have the following duties implied in their contracts:

- to obey lawful orders
- to exercise reasonable care and skill
- to show loyalty and good faith.

Illegal Exclusion Clauses

Employers cannot exclude or retract liability for death or personal injury to an employee caused by the employer's negligence. Any restriction on liability for other loss or damage caused by an employer's negligence must be "reasonable".

Changes in Contracts

Can the contract be changed?

An employer cannot impose any changes unilaterally. Any necessary changes should be in consultation with the employee. If an employee refuses to accept them, the employer can only change the contract by terminating it on due notice and offering re-engagement on new terms. It is possible for the employee to then claim unfair dismissal or breach of contract if the new terms are refused.

Can I be asked to teach a different subject from the one I was appointed to teach?

Teachers are usually prepared to accept changes to their curriculum programme or teaching load so long as the total required of them falls within the "directed time", but, occasionally, a Head can overstep the mark. It is not likely to be reasonable to ask an English teacher to teach Science or PE because of the possible safety risks. However, it is not uncommon for History teachers to teach English. It all comes down to the reasonableness of the Head's demands in context.

In *Redbridge v Fishman* (1978), an Industrial Tribunal had to decide whether it was reasonable for a new Head to require the head of the school's resources centre to teach 18 hours per week, when she had been appointed as a full-time teacher in charge of the resources centre, with only incidental duties. She was dismissed for refusing to obey the Head's instruction. The LEA argued that a teacher may be required to teach any subject at any time. The Employment Appeal Tribunal considered this proposition to be more "acceptable to Dotheboys Hall than a progressive London Borough". The Tribunal accepted that some flexibility is required but, save in emergencies, teachers can only be obliged to accept similar duties to those they have been doing.

Part-time Teachers

Part-time teachers have the same employment protection rights as full-time teachers, regardless of how many hours per week they work (see page 17).

Working Time

The school day for maintained schools is divided into two sessions, separated by a break in the middle of the day, except in exceptional circumstances. With the exception of nursery schools, all maintained schools must meet for 380 sessions per school year. Teachers have to be available to work for another five days, usually but not always for training purposes.

Changes to the timings of the start and finish of each day can only take effect from the beginning of a school year. The procedures for changing timings are laid down in the **Changing of School Session Times Regulations 1999**.

Changes to the structure of the school year, for example having five rather than three terms, have happened in some schools, particularly City Technology Colleges, and are under general discussion again nationally.

The *School Teachers' Pay and Conditions Document* (STPCD) also lays down the working time for full-time teachers. The working time of part-time teachers should be set out in the particular contract. Heads, members of the leadership group and advanced skills teachers (ASTs) are not subject to the time limits of teachers not in these groups.

Teachers, other than ASTs or members of the leadership group, employed full-time in a maintained school (but not teachers employed mainly in residential establishments) have to be available for work for 195 days in any year, of which 190 days are days on which the teacher may be required to teach pupils in addition to carrying out other duties. The use of the five non-teaching days is at the discretion of the Head, although the LEA may have a policy on the use of the days and may decide which days are designated as training days for its schools.

The maximum number of hours that a teacher can be required to work as a teacher under the direction of the Head, is 1265 hours which the Head must allocate reasonably throughout the year. Time spent in travelling to and from the place of work does not count towards the 1265 hours.

The duties to be performed will be those specified by the Head (and at times and places specified by the Head) for 1265 hours in any school year. The hours must be allocated reasonably throughout those days.

In addition, teachers are required to work such additional hours as may be needed to discharge their professional duties effectively. These duties include marking pupils' work, writing reports on pupils and preparing lessons, teaching materials and teaching programmes. The amount of time for this purpose beyond the 1265 hours cannot be defined by the employer, but depends on the time needed to complete the necessary work.

How do I know when my 1265 directed time is up?

The division of the hours between time directed for teaching and time for other duties is a matter for the Head. Heads are likely to issue a "time budget" setting out the division of time. Teachers are not noted for totting up hours and most are content to see that the division is reasonably equitable and that no serious changes are made during the year.

Can the Head direct me to work in a particular place?

A teacher must be available to teach or perform other reasonable duties at such times and places as may be specified by the Head (or the LEA, if not assigned to a particular school).

What happens if the workload is excessive?

A teacher's duties as laid down in Part XI of the *School Teachers' Pay and Conditions Document* are not limited to the working time prescribed in paragraph 40 (see above). Nevertheless, it may happen that the workload is seen to be excessive, in which case an individual teacher could discuss this with the head of department or Head and has a right to use the school's grievance procedures if necessary.

In Circular 2/98 *Reducing the Bureaucratic Burden on Teachers* the Secretary of State advised Heads in consultation with teachers to implement the advice offered in the circular to enable teachers to concentrate on improving the achievement of their pupils.

The case of *Wandsworth LBS v NASUWT* (1993) established that an excessive workload in relation to recording and reporting on pupils' progress can be the basis for a legitimate industrial dispute. The option of going to one's union representative is always open to a teacher. The union group in consultation with the union's staff will determine what advice to give.

In 2002 the School Teachers Review Body (STRB) published a *Special Review to Reducing Teacher Workload*. It made recommendations on:

- a guarantee of professional time
- embedding the place of continuing professional development
- moderating the impact of the requirement in the School Teachers' Pay and Conditions Document for Heads and governors to have regard to the statutory guidance in ensuring that teacher workloads are managed in ways which take account the demands of the job, but also respect the need to maintain a reasonable balance between work and home life.

Fast track teachers

The Fast Track Teacher Programme aims to develop teachers with excellent leadership potential early in their teaching careers, and to bring more of the brightest and best graduates and career changers into teaching. Its main attraction is to offer such candidates rapid career progression to expert teacher and leadership positions.

The programme is open to serving teachers, those on Initial Teacher Training (ITT) courses and those considering a career change from outside school teaching.

The first cohort of teachers on the programme will be drawn from two groups: those recruited from outside the profession who began ITT in September 2001; and serving teachers who were able to apply from November 2001.

The first teachers took up Fast Track posts in September 2002.

Eligibility of schools

Schools wishing to take part in the programme have to demonstrate that they can provide support and commitment to a teacher on the Fast Track Programme and that the Fast Track teaching post provides sufficient opportunity and challenge.

Midday breaks

No teacher is obliged to carry out supervisory duties during the midday break. This is now incorporated in the teachers' conditions of employment.

All supervision of school meals in dining rooms and around the site at midday is subject to schemes for midday supervision involving separate contracts.

Teachers may join in the scheme and be paid at a sessional or hourly rate, but it is more usual now to have persons other than teachers acting as supervisors. However, many teachers voluntarily take part in duties around the school at lunchtime or run school activities. They are covered by their employer's insurance at these times.

> *Can a teacher be directed to supervise during a midday break?*
>
> A teacher is entitled to a break of reasonable length either between the two sessions of the day or between the hours of 12–2pm. During this time a teacher cannot be required to supervise pupils.
>
> Schools can employ midday supervisors and teachers can enter into a separate contract as a midday supervisor on a voluntary basis. Teachers often volunteer to take extra-curricular activities during the break.

Does a teacher have any responsibilities if he or she remains on site?

Teachers can, and very frequently do, volunteer to take part in some supervision at midday break. Usually this takes the form of participating in the organisation of extra-curricular activities. Some schools provide free school lunches for staff who are involved in these activities.

All other teachers who remain on site at lunchtime have a residual duty of care. If they happen to see children in any kind of jeopardy, they have a duty to step in.

They also have a legal duty to see children safely in and out of classrooms into the care of the midday supervisors.

Schools should have clear schemes for lunchtime supervision.

It is in everyone's best interests for "a quiet afternoon" to see that lunch breaks are as free from undue excitement as possible.

Performance Management

A new performance management scheme is now in place and replaces the previous regulations for teacher appraisal. It centres on an annual review of each teacher's performance against agreed targets. The regulations apply to:

- teachers in maintained schools, other than those on contracts of less than one year or employed to work at more than two such schools
- qualified and unqualified school teachers
- teachers working full or part-time.

They do not apply to:

- teachers in their induction year
- teachers employed for less than one school year
- teachers employed centrally by the LEA.

However, schools are encouraged to consider how the performance review arrangements could be applied in a modified form to such teachers.

All schools are required to have a performance management policy, and the DfES has provided a model policy. Performance management is an ongoing cycle involving three stages.

1. Planning.
2. Monitoring.
3. Reviewing.

It will take place over one year, linking with the school's planning for school management, target-setting and budgeting processes. The precise timing will be decided within each school.

During the autumn term teachers will agree with their line managers personal targets for their teaching and other responsibilities. This will result in an "individual plan" recording the responsibilities and objectives as a basis for the performance review.

Each teacher's objectives should cover pupil progress and their own professional development. Management/leadership objectives will be appropriate, too, for teachers with these responsibilities. The scope of the objectives should be appropriate to the teacher's responsibilities.

Professional development targets might include observation of other teachers, mentoring, good practice development and training. In setting the objectives, account should be taken of the teacher's career aspirations.

The objectives should be clear and challenging.

During the year the teacher and his/her team leader should discuss progress towards the targets. Classroom observation should also be built into the process. The team leader must observe the teacher at least once during the year. Each school should set out the process of classroom observation clearly. Many schools use a standard pro-forma.

At the end of the year the teacher and team leader should reflect on the teacher's performance in a structured way. The focus should be on how to raise performance and improve effectiveness. In addition to the information obtained personally the team leader can obtain oral and written information from others, but must discuss this first with the reviewee.

It should involve:

- reviewing, discussing and confirming essential tasks
- recognising strengths and achievements
- confirming action agreed during informal discussions
- identifying areas for development
- recognising personal development needs.

A statement of the outcome of the review will be made by the team leader. A copy must be given to the reviewee within 10 days. The reviewee has a further 10 days to add comments, or make a complaint about the review statement to the Head. The completed review goes to the Head.

If the teacher moves to a new school during the cycle, he or she will move onto the new school's cycle, which will mean that the review will probably be less than one year.

Schools can call on nationally trained and accredited experts on performance management:

- *consultants* to advise on performance management policy and practice
- *advisors* to advise the governors on the Head's performance review and pay
- *assessors* to verify the Head's decisions on threshold applications (see below).

Guidance is provided in a document *Performance Management in Schools: Guidance Note*, April 2000, and *Performance Management Framework*, April 2000.

Is there a definition of a "good" teacher?

There have now been various attempts to define what a good teacher should know and do. OFSTED has its own definition and categories. According to OFSTED teaching skills are clustered under seven headings:

- planning
- time and resource management
- methods and strategies
- assessment
- pupil management/discipline
- homework
- high expectations.

OFSTED has also published guidelines on subject management. The Teacher Training Agency (TTA) has also published National Standards for Headteachers, Subject Leaders, Special Educational Needs (SEN) Co-ordinators, SEN Specialists and Qualified Teacher Status and Induction. The DfES has published the Standards for Advanced Skills Teachers and Threshold Assessment.

In addition the Government commissioned a private management consultancy firm, Hay McBer, to do research into the professional characteristics of a good teacher. The firm published in 2000 a report, *A Model of Effective Teaching*, which concluded that effective teaching depends on the following:

- teaching skills
- professional characteristics
- classroom climate.

The report suggests that good teachers demonstrate:

- professionalism (respect for others, challenge and support, confidence and creating trust)
- thinking skills (analytical and conceptual)
- planning and setting expectations (drive for improvement, initiative)
- leadership (managing pupils, passion for learning, flexibility, accountability)
- effective relationships with others (understanding, impact and influence, teamwork).

Health and Safety

Under health and safety legislation, LEAs and schools as employers have a duty to ensure that schools are safe places for employees and visitors. Employees too, have a duty to ensure their own safety and so far as is practicable, the safety of others. Schools have to have health and safety committees if requested to do so by a recognised union, but most schools have one anyway. Schools will also have a health and safety officer, sometimes the Head, but more often another member of the leadership group or other senior member of staff. Further details are included in Chapter 3.

"Topics in Safety" published by the Association for Science Education (ASE) encourages science teachers to do more practical work by helping them to take proper account of the risks and hazards involved. It gives authoritative advice and information. It can be obtained from ASE Booksales on telephone number 01707 283001.

Can I claim compensation if I am injured at work?

If you are injured at work then you can receive compensation for "industrial injuries" through an employer's normal insurance cover. If the employer has been negligent in any way then it is also possible to make a claim through the courts. A number of cases concern slipping on floors. In a recent non-school case, *Gilbert v John Wilman Ltd* (2000), a machine operator slipped on water left on a floor and twisted his knee badly enough for him having to stop his recreational fitness activity for which he had a history of awards and national publicity. He took redundancy and was awarded £8000 compensation.

Compensation might be reduced if the injured person is adjudged to have contributed to injury by his or her actions.

Stress

An employer's responsibility for the health and safety of employees includes caring for employees who are suffering from stress.

Heads have a duty to identify employees who may be vulnerable to stress. It is also up to the teacher to tell Heads when they are under stress. Headteachers should not be left to "second guess" the stress of the teacher. Guidance is given to Heads in the Health and Safety Commission's Education Service Advisory Committee booklet *Managing Occupational Stress: A Guide for Managers and Teachers in Schools* (HSE Books, 1995).

Guidance is also available in a booklet *Fitness to Teach* published by the Stationery Office, and in another booklet *Monitoring and Management of Sickness Absence in Schools* published by the National Employers' Organisation for School Teachers (NEOST).

What happens if a teacher cannot get into school because of mental stress?

If a teacher is suffering from stress, he or she should seek medical advice. The school should also be informed of the problem.

Teachers are likely in the first instance to approach their own doctor, but they could also approach the LEA's occupational health unit. The school or LEA may also refer the teacher to the unit during the process.

Schools should co-operate with the doctor in helping a teacher to get back into full employment. If this proves impossible then it is in both the school's and employee's interests to recognise the ill-health and the need either for a change of duties, where this is possible, or for the teacher to consider making an application to retire on the ground of ill-health.

Assaults on Teachers

The *Burgundy Book* deals with the injurious consequences of assault.

Any person who creates nuisance or disturbance to teachers, or others, on school premises, commits an offence under the **Education Act 1996**. This includes parents who use threatening or abusive words, or behave in a disorderly manner. If they persist they could be arrested.

Staff have a right to prosecute culprits. The police are normally willing to assist but do not usually prosecute common assaults.

Although employers (LEA or governors) have a duty to provide safe conditions, there is little they can do to prevent non-accidental injury. Employers can, however, assist victims. Civil action is costly, but the Criminal Injuries Compensation Authority will meet claims for compensation.

Staff rendered unfit for work after an assault are entitled to sick pay.

If the assault is by a pupil, the question arises whether the teachers can refuse to teach that pupil. No employer can ask employees to put themselves at risk. Where a serious risk is likely, a teacher has a right to refuse, but such occurrences will be extremely rare.

What should I do if accosted by an irate parent?

One of the most unnerving events for a teacher at any time in his or her career is to be faced with an irate parent. At that precise moment, the law does not help much. The best response if a few moments of reasonableness do not work is for the teacher to ask the parent courteously to accompany them to the Head or deputy head. The teacher should not enter into a slanging match. It is the Head's job to face up to these situations.

If things get out of hand, the Head may be able to have the parent removed from the site under s.547 of the **Education Act 1996**, which makes it an offence to create a nuisance or a disturbance on educational premises.

I am receiving threats from a parent. What can I do?

Your employer (the LEA or governors) should tell the parent that this must stop. The **Protection from Harassment Act 1997** makes it a criminal offence for a person to pursue a course of conduct which causes another harassment. It is a separate offence to pursue a course of conduct which causes another to fear that violence will be used against him or her. A restraining order can be issued by the court prohibiting further harassment or conduct which causes fear of violence.

The Act also creates a civil offence of harassment, allowing a victim to seek an order restraining the harasser without having to wait for police intervention. It is not much use if a parent suddenly bursts into a classroom, but it could help curb persistent troublemakers.

Harassment at Work

Increasingly, teachers have complained about harassment at work. It is usually women who feel at risk and it is usually some form of sexual innuendo which is the source of their complaint. However, it is not always so. Both men and women have complained of "bullying" by Heads or other staff making their lives intolerable in one form or another.

Any such kind of harassment is unlawful. It offends the Sex and Race Discrimination Acts, conditions of employment and Codes of Practice in the *Burgundy Book* (see page 10).

A teacher who feels aggrieved should not hesitate to take the matter up with his or her union, a senior colleague or the Head.

If there is no improvement, what do I do?

If the informal grievance procedure does not produce the desired outcome, a teacher would be entitled to complain formally to the Head and to expect the Head to set up a hearing to which the complainant, and accused will be invited. Both will be given a hearing and the Head should come to a conclusion quickly. If still not satisfied, the complainant could appeal to an appeal committee of at least three governors. At each stage, the complainant can bring in a union representative. The Head could institute formal disciplinary proceedings against the accused if the circumstances warrant it. This would be for the Head to decide.

A number of LEAs have produced model procedures dealing with bullying and harassment.

Ultimately, the teacher is entitled to take his or her case to an Employment Tribunal and through the courts, but in these circumstances it is likely that the union and/or one of the Commissions (EOC or CRE) will be involved.

Sick Leave

A teacher who is absent from school is deemed to be absent without cause until notification is given that the reason is illness. A teacher will normally be required to "self-certify" a sickness absence lasting for more than three days. This need not necessarily be done on the fourth day but completion of a form will normally be requested on return to work.

A doctor's certificate is normally required for any illness lasting longer than seven calendar days. This should be sent to the school on the eighth calendar day of absence.

A teacher whose absences are frequent or whose single absence is prolonged may be required at any time to submit to a medical examination at the employer's initiative. There is no definition of "prolonged", but the Government's requirements on the fitness of teachers have the effect that a medical examination is likely to be required after a three-month absence. Increasingly, employers are referring teachers to the Occupational Health service.

A teacher who is absent from a maintained school at the end of a half or full term because of an illness which then spreads into the holiday period should notify the school when he or she becomes fit. This enables the employer to make statutory sick pay (SSP) adjustments beneficial to them. Teachers in independent schools may be subject to the same requirement in their contracts.

Advice on sick pay is given in Chapter 3.

Capability Procedures

Under-performance can occur through a variety of reasons. There may be personal, private problems that make life difficult, or there may be professional problems. Skills can become outdated and interest becomes more difficult to sustain. The nature of a job can change and different demands be made of employees. It is no different in teaching.

How does a school identify under-performance?

Under-performance can be identified in a variety of ways, eg during the formal performance review process, through classroom observation, or not hitting agreed targets, or through informal discussion, or review of a teacher's lesson plans, marking, keeping up-to-date mark books, or sometimes via parent or pupil complaints. Whatever the initial trigger, the Head or manager has a duty to investigate the matter sensitively and to deal fairly and reasonably with the teacher concerned. That is why clear procedures have been drawn up.

The procedures

Schools must have by law procedures for dealing with lack of capability, and must have regard to any guidance from the Secretary of State. The Secretary of State issued such guidance in July 2000: *Capability Procedures for Teachers*, DfES 0125/2000.

Where a teacher is under-performing the Head, or other line-manager, must investigate and collect evidence. Once the facts have been obtained and the seriousness of the problem established the Head can decide to:

- drop the issue
- arrange additional training and support on an informal basis, including coaching and counselling
- arrange a formal interview.

Informal counselling should aim to encourage the teacher to improve and should be done discreetly. The teacher must be told:

- what is required
- how performance will be reviewed
- the review period
- and that formal procedures will be initiated if there is no improvement.

After a period of review involving observation and assessment the Head must come to a decision, whether to drop the issue or to convene a formal interview.

The formal stage

The formal interview initiates the formal stage. It allows the problems to be dealt with in a structured way. The teacher should be given at least five working days (or seven consecutive days out of term) notice of the date of the interview in order to prepare a response to the allegations. The teacher can be accompanied by a colleague or union representative.

At the formal interview the Head has four options:

- drop the matter
- counselling (except where this has already been done without improvement)
- oral or written warning
- final written warning.

The decision on which level of warning will depend on the seriousness of the problem. Only where the education of children is in jeopardy is it possible to move straight to a final written warning. This will then invoke an assessment period not exceeding four weeks.

Any appeal against a warning must be made within five working days (or seven consecutive days out of term), and heard within 10 working days (or 14 consecutive days out of term) of notification of appeal. The appeal cannot interrupt the progress of the procedure, unless the appeal decision leads to the matter being reconsidered.

If the Head issues a formal warning he or she should:

- identify the professional shortcomings
- give guidance on the standard required
- explain support that will be given
- explain the monitoring of performance over the following weeks
- identify a time-table for improvement
- agree a date for the next or final evaluation meeting
- make clear that failure to improve may lead to dismissal.

A letter recording the decision and discussion and giving information about the handling of the formal stage should be sent to the teacher immediately.

What happens when a warning has been issued ?

The "First Assessment" stage consists of 20 weeks of regular observation, monitoring and evaluation of performance. In week 20 an evaluation meeting will assess the performance over the previous weeks. If the performance has been satisfactory the procedures can end here.

If the performance is still unsatisfactory a final written warning should be issued. A "second assessment" stage will now commence. For four more weeks regular monitoring and evaluation will continue, with more guidance, training and support. In week 24 a final evaluation meeting will be convened to assess the teacher's performance.

If the performance is unsatisfactory the teacher must be told that the matter will be referred to the governing body's Staff Dismissal Committee. The result of the assessment and main points of the meeting should be recorded in a letter to the teacher.

Can a teacher appeal against formal warnings ?

Appeals may be heard by a senior manager, an LEA adviser or an individual governor. More governors might be used so long as this does not compromise the availability of governors for the Staff Dismissal and Appeal Committees. Appeals should normally be restricted to considering the reasonableness of the decision, any new evidence or any procedural irregularities.

The test for overturning a formal warning is that the decision was so unreasonable that it was one that no other Head or manager, acting with proper regard to his/her responsibilities, could have made.

If an appeal is upheld it should be referred back to the Head or manager to be further considered.

What happens if a teacher falls ill during the capability procedures ?

If long-term sickness appears to have been triggered by the commencement of the procedures the case should be referred to the employer's occupational health service, who will assess the teacher's fitness for continued employment. The service will guide the school on the length of time it would be reasonable to wait for a teacher's health to improve before considering the termination of a teacher's employment.

What kind of support can a teacher expect?

A teacher should be given feedback and guidance from those monitoring the performance in order to improve his/her performance. If a training course or assistance from within the school would help then this should be arranged as soon as possible. They should not, however, interrupt the timing of the procedures.

Can a teacher be accompanied by a colleague at all stages of the procedures?

A teacher should inform his/her union as soon as the procedures have begun, preferably at the informal stage, although the formal representation will take place at the formal assessment stage. There is a legal entitlement to be accompanied by a colleague or union representative at formal interviews and evaluation meetings, and dismissal and appeal hearings. The union representative has to be trained before they can act as a formal representative. If the teacher's chosen companion is not available on the proposed date of a meeting, and the teacher proposes an alternative that is reasonable and falls within five working days of the one proposed for the meeting, the school must rearrange the event to suit the teacher.

Dismissal committee stage

If the teacher's performance after the final warning has remained unsatisfactory the teacher will be told at the evaluation meeting that the matter will be referred to the governing body's Staff' Dismissal Committee. This committee will consist of at least three governors and will hear the recommendations of the Head, or other line manager, and any representations the teacher might wish to make.

The governing body will also have a Staff Appeal Committee to hear any appeal against a dismissal decision.

Are the time limits for the procedure fixed periods?

No, they are only recommended upper limits. The model procedure proposes an upper limit of two terms for formal assessment of staff capability. Serious cases can be dealt with in four weeks, where it is clear that an acceptable level of improvement is beyond the ability of the teacher.

Further Training and Development

Through their conditions of employment teachers have to review their methods of teaching and programmes of work, and to participate in arrangements for further training and professional development.

Teachers are normally keen to further their own careers through training. Schools will have someone charged with overseeing professional development to advise and guide colleagues.

The LEA advisory service is still available to aid in this but nowadays schools have to buy in their expertise.

Alternatively, schools can use the training grants (mainly the Standards Fund) that are awarded each year to buy in training from any other body. Gradually some quality control is being established via the accreditation of the Teacher Training Agency and OFSTED inspection. The DfES has launched a new strategy for Continuing Professional Development (CPD) in 2001 with an enhanced range of opportunities (see page 141).

Teachers should be aware that a part of all school budgets contains monies for training, some of which is specified in the grant, but much of which can be determined by the school.

EQUAL OPPORTUNITIES AND DISCRIMINATION

Employees have a right not to be discriminated against on grounds of sex, marital status, race, disability, for some trade union reasons or for carrying out health and safety activities. They also have a right to equal pay between men and women for like work of equal value.

Unlawful Discrimination

The **Sex Discrimination Act 1975** and the **Race Relations Act 1976** have similar provisions forbidding unlawful discrimination in recruitment, selection, access to promotion, benefits and training.

Discrimination can be either:

- *direct*, ie treating a person less favourably on account of sex, colour, race, nationality or ethnic origin
- *indirect*, ie applying a condition or requirement which is such that:
  - the proportion of the people of the same sex or race that can comply is considerably smaller than the proportion of people not of that sex or racial group who can comply
  - the condition or requirement cannot be shown to be justifiable

- the condition or requirement is to the detriment of that person because he or she cannot comply with it.

It is also unlawful to discriminate against married people or against someone who has set in motion discrimination proceedings.

Sex Discrimination

Are there any grounds where sex discrimination is lawful?

If being a man or a woman is a genuine occupational requirement, then discrimination is not unlawful. Being a man or woman is a genuine occupational qualification (GOQ) for jobs in the following circumstances.

1. Where, for reasons of physiology (excluding strength and stamina), the job calls for a man or woman.
2. Where the job requires a man or woman for reasons of decency or privacy.
3. Where the nature of the location makes it impracticable for the post-holder to live anywhere else other than in accommodation provided by the employer and the nature of the accommodation is such that the sleeping and sanitary arrangements do not allow privacy as between men and women and it is not reasonable to expect the employer to provide alternative accommodation.
4. Where the nature of the job requires a person of one gender because:
   - it is in part of an establishment for persons requiring special care
   - these persons are all men or all women
   - it is reasonable for the job not to be held by a man (or woman)
   - the post-holder provides individuals with services promoting their welfare or education, which are most effectively provided by a man (or woman)
   - the job is one of two held by a married couple.

The Equal Opportunities Commission (EOC) has published a code of practice for the elimination of discrimination on grounds of sex and marriage.

Am I allowed time off for ante-natal care?

All pregnant employees are entitled to time off with full pay in order to attend ante-natal appointments, regardless of their length of service or whether they are full-time or part-time.

Race Discrimination

Similar arrangements for genuine occupational qualification exist as in the **Sex Discrimination Act**. Where the post-holder can provide most effectively for persons of his or her racial group with personal services promoting their welfare and education, it is not unlawful discrimination.

The Commission for Racial Equality (CRE) has published a Code of Practice. This guide recommends that employers:

- develop an equal opportunities policy
- monitor selection decisions and monitor practice
- take positive action to encourage minority groups to apply for vacancies and promotion.

Race Relations (Amendment) Act 2000

The **Race Relations (Amendment) Act 2000** gives a specific duty to LEAs and schools to combat racial discrimination and to promote equal opportunities and good relations. Schools must publish written policies for the promotion of racial equality, and arrangements for assessment and monitoring. A Statutory Code of Practice on the Duty to Promote Race Equality was published by the Commission for Racial Equality (CRE) in May 2002. Maintained schools are among the public bodies required to discharge general and specific duties, but not independent schools, except where an independent school has a contract with a public body, which may impose explicit requirements on the contractor to secure compliance with the Code.

A Guide for Schools has also been published, available from The Stationery Office.

Collection of ethnic statistics

In order to learn more about the progress of teachers with different ethnic backgrounds, the DfES collects statistics. Schools are obliged to comply with the regulations and should negotiate with staff the handling of any personal or sensitive data.

Local publication of information will be made by LEAs in the case of maintained schools.

What do I do if I think I am being discriminated against on the grounds of sex or race?

A teacher should first of all discuss the complaint with the Head and union representative and, if no satisfactory outcome from the discussion is forthcoming, should progress through the formal grievance procedures.

When a teacher thinks he or she has grounds for believing that he or she is being discriminated against, whether on sex or race grounds, a questionnaire, obtainable from the Equal Opportunities Commission (EOC) or Commission for Racial Equality (CRE) can be passed to the Head or governing body (or LEA if the LEA is the employer). The questionnaires are long and detailed but the information allows the EOC or CRE to assess the case and to give advice. Any claim to an Employment Tribunal must be presented within three months of the act complained of.

Disability Discrimination

The **Disability Discrimination Act 1995** makes it unlawful to discriminate against a disabled person in:

- recruitment
- terms of employment
- promotion, training, transfer or other benefits if the employer treats a disabled employee less favourably than others and cannot show that this treatment is justified.

Employers have to make reasonable adjustments to premises to ensure the disabled are not disadvantaged.

The Act does not apply to organisations which employ fewer than 15 (originally 20) people. Therefore, small schools where the LEA is the employer are caught by the Act but small schools not under LEA control are not included.

However, as far as pupils are concerned, the **Special Needs and Disability Act 2001** extends the **Disability Discrimination Act 1995** to all schools, including those independent schools which are Designated Educational Institutions under the Act and, therefore, have to comply with its provisions.

The **Disability Discrimination Act 1995** completes a trilogy of anti-discrimination legislation alongside the **Sex Discrimination Act 1975** and the **Race Discrimination Act 1976**.

Disability in this context refers to a physical or mental impairment which has, or has had in the past, a substantial and long-term adverse effect on a person's ability to carry out normal, everyday tasks.

No express definition of physical impairment is given but any sight problem correctable by glasses or contact lens is not included. However, severe disfigurements can be treated as having a substantial effect on ability. Mental impairment must be a clinically recognised illness.

A *long-term* condition would have to last for 12 months or more, or be expected to last that long.

DfES Circular 3/97 *What the Disability Discrimination Act 1995 Means for Schools and LEAs* contains useful advice.

What are employers liable for?

Employers will be liable for any discrimination against such disabled persons in the fields of recruitment, promotion, training, working conditions and dismissal.

Are employers allowed to get away with discrimination in any way?

As with sex and race discrimination, employers can show that the disability discrimination was "justified", by proving that it was necessary in the circumstances.

This defence would be subject to a legal duty to try to overcome the effects by making reasonable alterations to working conditions.

Specialist equipment could be provided or different working conditions applied. It might be possible to swap classrooms, provide a mobile telephone for communication, provide training, or provide a reader, interpreter or possible supervision.

The emphasis in the Act is on "reasonableness", which also applies to cost implications.

Whistle-blowing

Employees are protected from victimisation by an employer if they reveal any wrong-doing or malpractice — popularly known as whistle-blowing. In making the disclosure the employee must be acting in good faith and must not commit a criminal offence, or disclose to an outsider any confidential information. A person who makes malicious allegations can be disciplined (**Public Interest Disclosure Act 1998**).

DISCIPLINARY AND GRIEVANCE PROCEDURES

All schools have staff disciplinary procedures drawn up by either the LEA or by the governors, after consultation with teacher unions or school staff.

The Advisory, Conciliation and Arbitration Service (ACAS) has produced a *Code of Practice on Disciplinary Practice and Procedures at Work.* The main points of the Code should also be reflected in a school's own procedures.

The procedures should:

- be in writing
- specify to whom they apply
- provide for matters to be dealt with quickly
- specify who has authority to take specific actions
- give opportunities for proper information to be given and for employees to be able to state a case
- give a right to be accompanied by a union representative or friend
- ensure that, except for gross breaches, no employee is dismissed for a first breach of discipline
- ensure no action is taken before careful investigation
- ensure full explanations for any penalty imposed
- provide a right of appeal and specify procedures.

Normally the procedures will take the following form.

Informal Warning

An informal warning would be given at an early stage to a teacher who is giving cause for concern. Support and help should also be provided.

Formal Oral Warning

This warning should be made in the presence of a senior member of staff. The teacher may also bring a friend or union representative to the meeting.

A record of the warning will be put on file and a statement must be made to the effect that any future breach may lead to the next phase of the disciplinary procedure.

Formal Written Warning

If circumstances warrant it, a further interview will take place conducted by the Head or LEA representative according to the procedure. This meeting will normally result in a formal written warning specifying that, if there is a further breach, a final written warning will be issued or, if this stage is also the final stage according to the procedure laid down, dismissal procedures may be set up.

Disciplinary Interviews

Before disciplinary warnings are given, a teacher should be called to a disciplinary interview. In the first instance, this is likely to be with the Head (who may be accompanied by a deputy head or other colleague) or in larger schools with a head of department or other senior member of staff. The teacher may also bring along a union representative or a friend.

The teacher should receive advance notification of the date and time of the interview, a written note of the complaint and the procedure to be followed.

The teacher must be informed of any witnesses to be called and should be provided with any witness statements taken. The teacher should inform the Head of any witnesses he or she wishes to call.

The **Employment Relations Act 1999** gives all employees the right to be represented at disciplinary meetings. If the teacher is accompanied by a union official it is likely that the Head will also seek representation. If the teacher is accompanied by a friend, it is desirable to establish at the outset who is doing the speaking.

A union representative taking on this role now should be trained in the role.

At the interview the complaint should be set out and procedures explained. The teacher must be allowed ample time to give his or her case and to call witnesses. If new facts emerge, it is possible for the hearing to be adjourned.

The Head may give a decision immediately or, in exceptional circumstances, may do so at a later date, where further investigation is necessary.

In the case of a warning, the teacher should be told clearly the reasons for the action, what improvements are necessary and by when, and the consequences if no improvement is made.

The decision will be confirmed in writing. The Head will also inform the teacher of his or her right of appeal to a committee of the governing body. Such appeals should be heard promptly — within 10 days as a guide.

A hearing of the appeal by the governors will follow the same format as the original disciplinary interview. The Head may be at the meeting, as a witness, but must withdraw during the decision-making process.

A further appeal is possible — against either a disciplinary decision or dismissal — to an appeal committee of the governing body. This committee will be different from the first committee and has a duty to examine the case afresh.

Settling Disputes and Grievances

All employers have to make clear to employees the means of settling grievances. Many problems are sorted out quickly between colleagues. Occasionally they are more serious or deep-rooted and the grievance procedures as laid down should then be used.

If I feel I am being treated unfairly, what should I do?

All schools will have grievance procedures, usually drawn up by an LEA on the basis of the model procedures set out in the *Burgundy Book.*

A teacher should first of all attempt to resolve the matter by a direct approach to the colleague or colleagues involved or through discussion with the head of department, professional tutor or other senior member of staff. A word with the union representative might also be helpful. This is a matter for the judgment of the aggrieved person.

Where an aggrieved person requests an interview with the Head or other colleague over a problem, it should be granted within five working days.

By mutual agreement, the senior member of staff can invoke the aid of others, but if the matter is not resolved, the aggrieved person can submit a formal notice of the grievance to the Head. In some cases, it will then be appropriate for the Head to formally notify the chair of the governing body (and the LEA). The governors (and officers of the LEA) may then try to resolve the matter.

Ultimately the governors can arrange a panel meeting to hear the grievance formally. At this stage, one is entitled to be represented if so wished. Reports should be made available by both sides and the panel should allow all parties to make their submissions, each of them accompanied by a friend or union official if they so wish.

Such a formal meeting should be arranged within 10 days of the breakdown of the informal procedures.

There is a right of appeal by any party to an appeal panel of the governing body, which cannot contain members from the original hearing.

There may be some variations to these model procedures in particular schools.

TERMINATION OF EMPLOYMENT

If dismissal is contemplated at the end of a disciplinary procedure, the teacher has the right to appear before a disciplinary committee of the governing body, which will operate according to the agreed procedures. The rules of natural justice apply, ie the teacher has a right to answer the charges, and no one on the panel should have been involved previously in the procedures. There is a right of appeal to another committee of the governors. No one from the first committee may sit on the appeal committee. There is no right of appeal to any other body, eg the LEA, but employees with at least one year's service have the right to take a case of unfair dismissal to an Employment Tribunal.

Unfair Dismissal

All employees who have at least one year's continuous service have a right not to be unfairly dismissed. Employees dismissed on some grounds, eg sex, pregnancy, race, disability, health and safety or trade union activities, need no qualifying service.

Under normal contracts, a teacher should receive two months' notice in the spring and autumn terms and three months' notice in the summer term, terminating at the end of the term. Heads receive three and four months' notice respectively. All employees are entitled to receive a minimum of one week's notice for each year of service up to a maximum of 12 weeks' notice.

Part-time and fixed term teachers must now be treated in the same way as full-time teachers. After four years of successive fixed term contracts a teacher will be deemed to have full-time status, unless the employer and employees have reached a collective agreement on a limit to the use of successive fixed term contracts.

Fair Dismissal

The reasons for a fair dismissal must fall into one of five categories.

1. Dismissal can be on the grounds of capability or qualifications.
2. There can be a reason related to conduct.
3. It can be due to redundancy.
4. It can be due to the contravention of a duty or restriction imposed by an Act of Parliament.
5. It can be because of some other substantial reason of a kind justifying the dismissal, eg unreasonable refusal to take another subject or change hours of work.

Once a category has been established, an Employment Tribunal would have to consider that the decision was reasonable in the circumstances.

Most important in this context are the procedures used during the dismissal proceedings.

Tribunals will expect the ACAS Code of Practice and any other agreed procedures to have been followed.

Where the ground is lack of capability, it will have to be shown that no unreasonable demands were made and that relevant help and training were given.

In the case of gross misconduct, most of the stages of the disciplinary procedures will be bypassed. The dismissal procedures will be invoked. This may also happen in the case of gross incompetence.

Part-time Teachers

Part-time teachers cannot be dismissed simply to aid curriculum reform or to reduce staff, without taking into consideration their right to claim unfair dismissal.

If the hours of a part-time employee with statutory entitlement are "significantly" reduced this may be regarded as a dismissal and could lead to a claim for unfair dismissal. There is no formal definition of "significant", but more than a 20% reduction in hours might be considered unfair.

Misconduct

The Secretary of State has powers to prevent or restrict the employment of a person in a school on the grounds of misconduct whether or not the misconduct has resulted in a conviction for a criminal offence. The Secretary of State can make a "direction", which could:

- require an employer to terminate employment
- prohibit a person's employment in a relevant occupation
- impose specific conditions on the continuing employment.

In certain cases where a person has been found guilty of a sexual offence involving a child under 16, a direction is automatic. These include rape, unlawful sexual intercourse, indecent assault and gross indecency.

Apart from these automatic barrings, the person concerned must be given the opportunity to make representations before a decision is reached.

Further information on the Secretary of State's power to bar persons is given in DfES Circular 11/95 *Misconduct of Teachers and Workers with Children and Young Persons.*

What is gross misconduct?

This is behaviour which is well outside anything normally found in a school and is such that it will break the relationship of trust and confidence that must exist between an employer and employee. It may also have brought the school into considerable disrepute. The behaviour complained of is most likely to concern sexual or financial irregularity.

Misconduct is normally brought to the attention of the DfES by police or employer reports. The Secretary of State then has to decide whether the person is unsuitable for teaching.

The usual types of misconduct are sexual offences and violence, drugs-related offences and misappropriation of school funds — but there are others.

Barring from Employment

The Secretary of State has the power to bar people from, or impose conditions on their employment either as a teacher or in any other capacity. The prohibition can be for:

- medical reasons
- misconduct
- unfitness to be employed in work that brings him or her into contact with children
- being placed on the Secretary of State for Health's list of people considered unsuitable to work with children.

There is automatic barring of a person convicted of a sexual offence involving a child under 16, and for a number of other sexual offences.

Other cases likely to result in barring are:

- violent behaviour towards children
- drug related offences
- misappropriation of school property
- deception
- conviction resulting in a sentence of more than 12 months.

The **Sexual Offences (Amendment) Act 2000** created a new offence of "abuse of trust". This makes it an offence for a person over 18 to have any sexual activity with someone under 18 if in a position of trust to that person. Clearly this includes teachers and other school staff.

Referral to the General Teaching Council

The Secretary of State now has the power to refer certain cases concerning allegations of unacceptable professional misconduct, or where the teacher has been convicted of a relevant offence which has not involved the safety and welfare of children, to the General Teaching Council (GTC). The Council has the power to restrict the employment of a person in a school, or to bar them from teaching in a particular type of school, eg restrict them to teaching in a secondary school.

What happens to people who are found guilty of such an offence?

A person who has been deemed by the Secretary of State to be unsuitable for working with children is placed on a confidential list known as List 99. The list is issued annually to LEAsand other bodies.

Will I be sacked if I am convicted of an offence?

It all depends on the nature and circumstances of the offence. A teacher convicted of misappropriating school funds may well be dismissed as this directly affects his or her professional life. However, a teacher convicted of shoplifting or drunken driving is not likely to be dismissed as a result of this criminal activity. These are part of a teacher's private life and a school could be challenged if it invaded that privacy.

The test is whether the criminal behaviour is such that it is likely to directly affect the ethos and reputation of the school and, above all, the education and well-being of the pupils. The dilemma is most often apparent in cases involving sexual misconduct.

In *Nottinghamshire C.C. v Bowly* (1978), a teacher won his case in a Tribunal against dismissal following a conviction for indecency in a public place. The LEA, however, won the appeal. The Tribunal had considered that there was no evidence to suggest a risk to pupils at the school. The Employment Appeal Tribunal, however, considered that it was "difficult to say there was no risk".

In *Norfolk C.C. v Barnard* (1979), a Tribunal which reinstated a teacher dismissed for a criminal conviction involving drugs said that a dismissal is justified if a conviction for an offence outside employment seriously and genuinely affects his or her relationship with fellow employees and makes the employee a danger to children. Subsequent cases have tended to follow this test.

Suspension

The governing body and the Head have the power to suspend a teacher on full pay if his or her exclusion is required.

A hearing to consider the suspension should be held within 10 working days, and the teacher has the right to bring a union representative or friend to the hearing.

A suspension can only be ended by the governing body.

On what grounds can a teacher be suspended?

In an emergency, usually when a serious allegation has been made, a teacher can be suspended from duty.

The circumstances are likely to be either that a criminal charge is imminent or that the nature of the alleged offence suggests that children might be at risk or a major disruption in staff relations might occur.

The teacher has a right to know the reasons for the suspension, and the length of time the suspension will last. The suspension will be on full pay and will be carried out by the Head or governors.

Redundancy

Since the advent of local management of schools, redundancy has become commonplace as schools rarely have anywhere to redeploy teachers to. Some LEAs have introduced voluntary schemes but they remain marginal.

Redundancy is a form of dismissal and employers must have regard to the requirements of the **Employment Rights Act 1996**.

What is the definition of "redundancy"?

Dismissal by reason of redundancy occurs when the dismissal is wholly or mainly attributable to the following.

1. The requirements of the business (school) that employees carry out work of a particular kind, or carry out that work in the place that they were employed, have come to an end or lessened or are expected to do so, eg a change in curriculum balance due to the introduction of the National Curriculum and curriculum adjustment, an organisational restructure or falling pupil numbers.
2. Instances where the employer intends to cease, or has ceased, to carry on the business for which the employee was employed, eg school closure or significant reorganisation.

How can a governing body show that it has been "reasonable"?

In order to establish that it has acted reasonably, a governing body would need to:

- give as much warning as possible to an employee of its intentions
- ensure that its procedures and committee structures are in place
- establish the criteria to be used in selecting employees for redundancy in consultation with the relevant trade union(s) or employee representatives and seek agreement on the criteria
- ensure that the criteria, as far as possible, are objective and can be checked against such criteria as curriculum requirements, skills and level of qualifications required, organisation requirements, levels of responsibility, efficiency, length of service, etc (**Note:** great care must be taken to avoid identification by race, gender, marital status or trade union membership)
- consider any representation by the trade unions or employee representatives on the selection criteria
- employ all the strategies that might avoid compulsory redundancy, eg internal reorganisation (internal redeployment), reduction of hours (banning overtime), retraining of employees to enable them to meet the requirements of vacant internal posts, restrictions on recruitment, use of temporary, short-term, part-time contracts, establishing whether any employee would volunteer for redundancy or seek early retirement
- see whether alternative work can be offered within the LEA.

It is possible to make a pregnant employee redundant using the redundancy selection criteria *provided that her pregnancy is ignored.*

What are the processes for making teachers redundant?

It is important that LEAs and schools have policies and procedures laid down following consultation with employees (usually through union representatives). Once the possibility of redundancy is established, school management must:

- weigh up options
- get the views of staff
- make proposals to unions in writing
- ask for voluntary redundancies and early retirement
- decide who must go
- consult the employee(s) on the proposed redundancy
- try to redeploy affected employees
- ensure there is no breach of statutory rights
- offer help to find other work and allow time off to seek other employment.

The aim is to act fairly at all stages. All employees involved should have the right to representation and an employee selected for redundancy must have the right of appeal.

Does my school have a duty to find me alternative work if I am redundant?

The employer (LEA or school) has a duty to do all that is reasonably practicable to avoid making staff redundant including internal redeployment, reduction of hours, retraining, restrictions in recruitment and so on.

Employers also have a duty to try to find alternative employment for redundant teachers outside their present school. Time off must be allowed to enable them to find alternative employment.

Employers must act all through the processes as "a good employer".

LEAVE OF ABSENCE

Employee Rights

Employees have a statutory right to time off work in certain circumstances. LEAs and schools also have policies for time off in other non-statutory circumstances.

Time Off Work With Pay

Employees are entitled to take reasonable time off work, with pay, for the following purposes.

Trade union duties

Employers must allow officials of independent trade unions recognised by them to take time off work, with pay, to carry out relevant duties and to undergo training in respect of their duties.

Duties must be concerned with either negotiations in respect of which the union is recognised by the employer or any other duties sanctioned by the employer. In either event, the duties must be concerned with matters which fall within the definition of a trade dispute, eg terms and conditions, engagement or termination, allocation of work, disciplinary matters, union membership, facilities for union officials and negotiating machinery.

Requests for time off should be viewed according to the individual circumstances of the official concerned. The amount of time off to be given is whatever is reasonable in the circumstances, taking account of when and for what purpose it is required. Employers are not bound to give permission for time off when the absence will cause damage to the service/school which could be avoided by granting it at a different time. However, it must be noted that Appendix V of the *Burgundy Book* and most locally negotiated agreements define many of the matters referred to above and should be referred to by Heads when time off work is requested.

Heads, on behalf of the employer, must assess the reasonableness of the request, having regard to the *Burgundy Book* or other agreements and in light of the following factors:

- the purpose for which time off is requested
- the amount of time off required
- the occasions on which it is required
- any conditions subject to which time off may be taken, ie advance warning and availability of other employees to cover the work.

Further guidance is given in the ACAS *Code of Practice on Time Off for Trade Union Duties and Activities*.

If a teacher or other employee or, indeed, the Head is refused time off or payment, the matter can be placed before an Employment Tribunal. If the refusal is unreasonable, the Tribunal must:

- make a declaration

- order the employer to pay the amount that it considers is just and equitable having regard to the employer's default and the employee's loss
- where pay has been refused, award the pay due to the employee.

In practice, custom normally dictates the amount of time which the school considers can reasonably be taken for such purposes.

Looking for work or retraining

Employees who have been continuously employed for two years or more and are dismissed as redundant must be given reasonable time off to arrange training or a new job. Compensation of up to two-fifths of a week's pay (ie roughly two days' pay) can be awarded by an Employment Tribunal to an employee who is not allowed this time off.

Seeking work can include perusal of newspapers in the local library or a door to door search. There is no need for proof of appointments. Payment is based on what the employee would have earned if he or she was at work during his or her contractual hours.

Ante-natal care

A woman who is pregnant and has made an appointment to receive ante-natal care on the advice of a registered medical practitioner, registered midwife or registered health worker has the right to take time off with pay to keep the appointment provided that, if her employer requests it, she produces evidence of the appointment and, except for the first appointment, produces a certificate stating that she is pregnant.

Trade Union Activities

Is there a limit to the time off I can have as a union official?

The test is whether the time-off is "reasonable".

In one case, *Luce v London Borough of Bexley*, a teacher who was a local branch official of his union requested time off to attend a mass lobby of MPs over the Education Reform Bill. The request was turned down and he took the case to an Industrial Tribunal, which held that the lobbying did not constitute genuine union activity. The Employment Appeal Tribunal (EAT) agreed, saying that while it would be wrong to construe "union activity" too narrowly, some link between employer and trade union must exist. The lobbying of Parliament for plainly ideological purposes was not reasonable under the meaning of the Act.

Employee Representatives

An elected employee representative must be allowed reasonable time off work with pay to perform his or her function if there are proposed redundancies or a transfer of undertakings.

Public Duties

Employees who are Justices of the Peace, members of local authority councils, members of boards of prison visitors, members of a police authority, statutory tribunal members, National Rivers Authority members, health authority members or members of a National Health Service Trust, school, college or higher education corporation governors must be allowed reasonable unpaid time off to perform their duties (**Employment Rights Act 1996**). The duties include attendance at meetings or any other occasion approved by the body for the purpose of discharging their functions.

It must be noted that these are the minimum statutory provisions. National and local agreements provide better conditions and reference must always be made to these, eg *Burgundy Book* paragraphs 9.3–9.6, Appendices IV and V.

The amount of time off depends on what is reasonable in all the surrounding circumstances having regard to:

- how much time is required to perform the duties
- how much previous time off the employee has been allowed under this heading and for trade union duties and activities
- the circumstances of the employer's business and the effect the absence will have.

Such factors as the size of the operating unit, current workload difficulties, availability of cover, disruption for other employees and the essential nature of the employee's duties (the ability to make up lost time) could be borne in mind.

A Tribunal can award compensation to an employee in respect of failure to allow time off but it has no power to order the number of days that the employee is entitled to receive.

Jury Service

Teachers are not exempt from jury service. They can, however, in common with anyone who is called, ask to be relieved of the duty if summoned. Courts will only grant exemption for good reasons, although they should be sympathetic if the summons is at a sensitive time when the absence of a teacher is likely to cause particular damage to children's education. Teachers should write to the court explaining what the circumstances are.

Maternity Leave

The **Maternity and Parental Leave, etc Regulations 1999** sets out the minimum statutory rights. National agreements provide for enhancement of these for teachers in maintained schools, and in those independent schools which have adopted them.

The **Employment Act 2002** has enhanced maternity provision. (For details of the teacher scheme see page 86).

Parental Leave

The **Employment Relations Act 1999** introduced the right of all employees to take up to 13 weeks' parental leave to look after a child or make arrangements for a child's welfare. It applies to both mothers and fathers, who have or adopt a baby, provided they have completed one year's qualifying service with their employer.

The leave amounts to 13 weeks in total per child (eg if there are twins each parent is entitled to 13 weeks per child), *pro rata* for part-time teachers. The leave may be taken at any time up to the child's 5th birthday (or in the case of adoption up to the 5th anniversary of the date of adoption, up to the child's 18th birthday). It is not necessary for the parent to be living with the child in order to take the leave.

The leave must normally be taken in multiples of one week with a maximum of four weeks in any one year. Parents of disabled children must take the leave in multiples of one day but can take the leave up to the child's 18th birthday. In all cases 21 days' notice must be given.

The employer has the right to postpone the leave for up to six months if the school would be unduly disrupted, but this has to be discussed with the teacher first.

The leave is unpaid, but local agreements can provide for pay.

Dependant Leave

The **Employment Relations Act 1999** gave employees the right to take reasonable time off in connection with certain unexpected or sudden emergencies involving dependants.

Dependants are defined as: a spouse, a partner, a child, a parent and a person who lives in the same household as the employee, other than as his or her employee, tenant, lodger or boarder. In addition time off is allowed when the "dependant" is anyone who reasonably relies on the employee for assistance when he or she falls ill.

The time off can be taken for a variety of reasons, which amount to dealing with injuries, illness and other kinds of problem associated with care. Employees have to notify the employer of the reason as soon as reasonably practicable.

No set time off is specified in the legislation. The circumstances of the emergency will dictate what a reasonable amount of time off should be. There is, however, no obligation on an employer to pay the employee on dependant leave.

An employee who is thought to be abusing this statutory right is subject to the normal disciplinary proceedings.

Paternity Leave

The **Employment Act 2002** provides male teachers with a maximum of two weeks' paid paternity leave for employees whose partner has an expected week of birth on or after 6 April 2003.

Adoption leave will also be available to employees for children adopted after 6 April 2003.

Absenteeism

Absenteeism can be a great financial embarrassment to schools since the school or LEA has not only to continue to pay a full salary for short illnesses but also has to pay for cover.

Absences take a number of forms.

1. *Long-term absence* is usually because of long-term illness. Guidelines are laid out in the *Burgundy Book* and a number of LEAs now have their own procedures.
2. *Short-term absence* can be either authorised (for agreed reasons, usually set out in staff handbooks) or unauthorised (absence without excuse, or with false excuses). Persistent short-term absence occurs when staff are absent for a single day or for a few days here and there. Sometimes this is a symptom of stress and possible medical problems. Sometimes it is plain malingering.

It is important to note that all unauthorised absence is a breach of contract and, while most absence should be treated with sympathy and sensitivity, a balance has to be struck between concern for the teacher and concern for the pupils.

Consequently, schools will have procedures for identifying absence problems. They will require sick notes and eventually doctors' certificates and, if absence is persistent, they will require a satisfactory explanation. In the case of long-term illness the case should be referred to the occupational health service. The governing body will consider any advice given by the occupational health service on the fitness of the teacher to return, but it is ultimately the governors' decision on whether to institute dismissal proceedings. To aid them the governors can also request a teacher's agreement to a second medical opinion arranged by the school or LEA.

Before any dismissal proceedings are initiated, a teacher will be warned that dismissal might follow if further absence occurs.

Employers must consider possible alternative employment for employees unable to carry out their usual tasks through illness. In practice, it is rare for this to be possible for a teacher. Sickness benefit is considered in the section Sick Pay (Chapter 3, Teachers' Pay).

If I am under 60 and medically unfit to teach, what are my entitlements?

Teachers who are under 60 and are members of the Teachers' Superannuation Scheme are entitled to a lump sum payment and a pension if they have to retire early on the grounds of ill-health. Teachers' Pensions, the agency which administers the scheme, can have a teacher examined by its own advisors if necessary.

WORK EXPERIENCE

It is normal for secondary school pupils to spend some time in business during school hours between the ages of 14 and 18. The period is usually 1–3 weeks.

Under the *School Teachers' Pay and Conditions of Service Document*, a teacher can be required by the Head to visit the pupil at the place of work, since the Head can specify the places at which a teacher should be available. A teacher could only refuse on the ground that the direction was unreasonable. This might be because there was no transport or it took too long to get there or there was no reimbursement of expenses. Any such argument should be taken through the normal grievance procedures.

TRADE UNIONS

Employees' Right To Belong

All employees have a right to belong to a trade union, but the law only provides specific rights to trade unions and their members when they are recognised by an employer for negotiating purposes. Governing bodies of LEAmaintained schools must recognise all unions recognised by the LEA, but may also recognise other unions if they wish.

Independent schools, City Technology Colleges and City Academies may determine which unions they will recognise.

Employees' rights, briefly, are:

- to be consulted if redundancies are to be imposed
- for representatives to take time off work in connection with union duties (see page 64)
- to be given certain information
- to hold certain ballots on the employer's premises provided it is reasonably practicable.

Trade Disputes

Trade disputes (ie strikes or industrial action short of strikes) between employers and employees only attract immunity from civil actions for damages if they have been approved in a secret ballot and relate wholly or mainly to:

- conditions of employment
- engagement or suspension of employment
- allocation of duties
- discipline
- membership of a trade union
- facilities for trade unions
- consultation machinery.

Industrial action may be organised by a school staff against the governing body of the school with "immunity" if it follows from a majority result in a secret ballot held at the school.

If a recognised trade union wishes to hold a ballot for a decision on calling or ending a strike, or a decision on acceptance or rejection of an employer's proposal regarding conditions of employment, they have a right to use the employer's premises, on request, so long as it is reasonably practicable.

Disputes could be settled through ACAS but it is possible to have a binding compromise agreement between unions and employers without involving ACAS, where these relate to unfair dismissal, redundancy, discretion and salary disputes (**Employment Rights Act 1996**).

Facilities For Union Representatives

Employing authorities and teachers' organisations have agreed on the facilities that representatives of teachers' organisations in a school should enjoy. Many of the rights are also contained in the **Employment Rights Act 1996**.

Industrial Action

No employee has a "right to strike" in UK law. What is provided is immunity to members of trade unions from civil liability for certain actions carried out in the course of an industrial dispute.

The immunity arises when:

- the action has been endorsed by the members in a pre-action ballot
- the dispute relates to one or more specified issues relating to terms and conditions of employment
- the dispute is between employees and their own employer.

In *Wandsworth LBS v NASUWT* (1993), the Court of Appeal held that a dispute of "excessive workload" arising from the National Curriculum assessment and testing which was between the union and Secretary of State nevertheless came under the concept of a dispute arising from conditions of service of union members.

The **Employment Relations Act 1999** contains a provision giving employees the right to complain of unfair dismissal if the reason for dismissal is participation in protected industrial action.

Personal Data

Under the **Data Protection Act 1998** teachers (and all other employees) have the right to see any personal information on him or her which is kept by the school and/or the LEA, whether stored on paper files or in a computer. There are important exemptions, such as medical reports, information about actual or suspected child abuse, and references given for the purposes of education, training or employment.

The employee is not required to give his or her consent to the data being kept on file, unless it is sensitive information.

Most schools will already have a policy giving teachers access to their files. It is normal for staff to give notice of their request and for a senior member of staff to be present when the teacher peruses the information. There is no right to remove a file or any of its contents without permission.

Any exempted information can be kept on a separate file.

CHAPTER 3

TEACHERS' PAY

The Government has introduced a new system for Heads' and teachers' pay in the maintained sector. The new arrangements are set out in the School Teachers' Pay and Conditions Document (STPCD) and the accompanying guidance.

THE SYSTEM

Under the new system, teachers will be in one of the following groups for salary purposes:
- the leadership group and paid on the leadership spine
- Advanced Skills Teachers
- teachers on the main scale or upper pay spine.

The Leadership Spine

Teachers who hold senior posts and have whole-school strategic responsibilities, will be on the leadership spine, and will have the title of headteacher, deputy headteacher or, the new title, assistant headteacher.

Governing bodies will choose an appropriate five-point range from the spine for each assistant head (they do not have to be the same range for all assistant heads). The range for deputy heads in the school (also five points) will be at least one point higher than that of the highest paid assistant head, but the range for an assistant head can overlap with a deputy's range.

Progression up the leadership spine will be subject to the performance management review policy.

Advanced Skills Teachers

Advanced Skills Teachers (ASTs) are appointed mainly because of the quality of their teaching performance over a period of time. They are required to undertake in-service training with other teachers in the school or other schools. They are paid on a five-point range chosen by the governing body.

Fast Track Teachers

It is assumed that, provided high levels of performance are maintained, Fast Track teachers will reach the pay threshold at an accelerated rate. They will be able to access additional opportunities for continuing professional development.

The Main and Upper Scales

Every teacher not in the leadership group is either on a main scale of six points or beyond this threshold on an upper scale of a further five points. Teachers with QTS will be placed on point one of the main scale and will move up the scale incrementally each year to point six.

Teachers can receive additional points for their qualifications, or experience (eg relevant experience prior to becoming a teacher), double-jumping performance points and any additional allowance awarded to a fast-track teacher.

Additional Allowances

In addition teachers will be able to receive allowances for:

- extra management responsibilities
- special educational needs
- posts for which it is difficult to recruit teachers
- posts for which it is difficult to retain teachers.

An additional point can be awarded where a teacher has demonstrated excellent performance over the previous year, especially in relation to their classroom teaching.

Management allowances

There are currently five allowances. For each allowance there must be a clearly defined job description. They are not performance bonus payments.

Similar responsibilities should be rewarded at the same rate, and a teacher who has more than one responsibility will be allocated a management allowance two, three, four or five depending on the number of responsibilities and the relative weighting of the post. The head of a large department may receive a management four allowance, while a teacher who is, say, an assistant head of year and is also the work experience co-ordinator may receive a two or, in a bigger school, a three.

Special educational needs

Special educational needs (SEN) teachers can be considered for any of the other extra allowances, but can also be awarded one allowance if he or she is:

- teaching in a special school
- teaching in an ordinary school with wholly or mainly students with statements of special educational needs, whether or not in special classes
- teaching classes wholly or mainly made up of children who are hearing or visually impaired, even if they do not have statements.

Governing bodies can also award discretionary allowances to other teachers engaged in teaching wholly or mainly SEN pupils who do not have statements.

Teachers can also receive a discretionary "second allowance" where the relevant body (the governors or LEA) considers that his or her qualifications or experience merit it.

Some teachers may not have formal SEN teaching qualifications but may have acquired high quality expertise, such as signing for hearing impaired pupils.

Recruitment and retention

Governing bodies can award up to five allowances for a teacher of a subject in which there is a shortage or where posts are difficult to fill.

The governing body can award the allowance in a lump sum at the end of the year if it so wishes but not if the service in the previous year has been unsatisfactory.

Safeguarding

During the period of transition teachers are protected from the effects of moving from the pre-2001 structure. For example, teachers who held permanent half points in the old system will continue to retain the cash value.

Crossing the Threshold

Qualified teachers in the maintained sector who are already on point six of the main scale can apply to cross the threshold to the upper scale.

If the application is successful the teacher will be promoted to the first point of the upper pay scale. Teachers who do not apply when they reach point nine, or who are unsuccessful, can apply in future years.

In order to cross the threshold eligible teachers must demonstrate:

- knowledge and understanding — a thorough and up-to-date knowledge of the teaching of their subject
- teaching and assessment — consistent and effective planning of lessons, use of appropriate strategies and classroom management and knowledge of pupils' progress
- pupil progress — pupils are achieving well as a result of their teaching
- wider professional effectiveness — taking responsibility for their professional development and contributing to the policies and aspirations of the school
- professional characteristics — being effective professionals who challenge and support pupils to do their best.

External assessors have been trained and will visit the school to verify the Head's decisions about threshold applications on a sampling basis. It is expected that unsuccessful applicants will receive feedback to inform their future professional development needs. Teachers should also have the right to appeal against decisions to a second assessor or another body.

Guidance is provided by the DfES in a *Threshold Assessment Pack*.

Moving up the Upper Pay Spine

Further progression on the upper pay spine is not incremental. In 2002 teachers on the first point were eligible to move to the second point on the recommendation of the Head, based on "sustained and substantial" contribution to the school.

Weekend or Holiday Payments

Teachers who undertake in-service training at weekends or in school holidays (but not after the end of the school day) do so voluntarily and may receive a payment at the discretion of the governors. The guidance suggests that the amount paid should reflect the saving made from the supply cover budget.

Teachers in the leadership group and ASTs are not eligible, nor are part-time teachers, but in their case extra payments could be made through a separate contract or an extension of their existing one.

Can a teacher be paid for in-service training done in the evening?

For full-time teachers, INSET payments can only be made for INSET outside directed time, ie the 195 days on which a teacher is required to be available for specified work.

This means that any INSET organised after normal school hours in "twilight sessions" could not be paid for.

Full-time teachers cannot be required to take part in INSET outside directed time, nor can part-time teachers be required to do so outside the time when they are normally required to teach.

Governors and Heads are expected to respect the right of individuals to make their own choice, and to have a regard for equal opportunities.

It is usual for Heads to reach some general agreement with the staff on this issue as well as respecting individual teachers' rights.

What amounts should a teacher receive for voluntary INSET?

The relevant body (usually the governing body) must determine the activity for which teachers may be paid and the appropriate level of payment.

Since the overall aim is to reduce the number of hours that teachers are absent from the classroom, the payments should be met from savings on the supply cover budget and on the training budget.

No separate contract is required for this training. All such payments will be subject to income tax and national insurance contributions. All payments made under the Pay and Conditions Document are pensionable.

Payment for Initial Teacher Training Activities

Teachers who take part voluntarily in Initial Teacher training (ITT) activities (but not as part of their AST duties) may receive extra payments at a level which will reflect the amount received from the partner higher education institution. In some cases administrative duties connected with the ITT will be incorporated in a separate non-teaching contract.

What activities might be paid for?

The Government suggests that the supervision and observation of teaching practice, giving feedback to students, acting as mentors, running seminars on aspects of the course and formally assessing competencies would be suitable activities which can be regarded as an ordinary incident in the conduct of the school and which have always taken place in schools. Teachers could, therefore, be obliged to take part in these activities as part of a teacher's contract. Payment may be made for these activities as part of a teacher's job.

However, for other aspects of ITT which are not part of a teacher's job, a separate non-teaching contract of employment covering these aspects of involvement would be appropriate.

Such activities include the additional requirement of school-centred IT (SCITT) where schools take the lead in providing ITT, and the planning of an ITT course, preparing course materials, marketing, finance and administration of the course and the responsibility for the tuition and award of qualifications.

What amount could a teacher expect to receive?

This is a matter for the relevant body in the light of the school's financial circumstances and the money available from partnership with a higher education institution. The school's own budget can be used for ITT activities which are an ordinary incident in the conduct of the school.

The level of payment should be covered in the governors' salary policy.

School Achievement Award

Schools that are performing well or improving rapidly can now receive a *school achievement award* to pay for staff bonuses. The value of the award depends on the number of pupils in the school. The money is given to the school, the amount depending on the size of the school. It would be up to the school to decide how to allocate it, but everyone who works at the school, including all teachers and support staff, would be eligible.

The payments do not count towards teachers' pensions.

Fees Paid to Teachers

Teachers quite often receive payment for writing books, giving lectures, marking and moderating examination papers and so on. If the payment received is for work during school time or using school equipment or materials, a teacher should notify the Head of the circumstances. These activities are usually welcomed but it is proper for the Head to know about them and approve them if the teacher's work in the school could be affected. It is possible that all or part of a fee should be paid to the school or LEA.

What happens if I attend examiners' meetings in school time?

Examiners, assessors and moderators in external examinations are often called upon to attend meetings in school time. The school usually receives an agreed amount from the Board to cover any supply costs. Teachers will receive personally any expenses incurred.

Notification of Salary

Governing bodies must assess each teacher's points situation as at 1 September each year, or when taking up a post. They *may* also make an assessment at any other time, eg in awarding management allowances. Teachers should then be given a written statement of the points and allowances assessment showing:

- the points assessed, allowances awarded and whether temporary or permanent
- any safeguarded points held
- any extra or bonus payments
- the total salary position.

Unattached Teachers

The remuneration of an unattached teacher (ie one who is held on the staff of the LEA and is not on the complement of any particular school) is determined in accordance with whichever provisions of the Pay and Conditions Document the relevant body considers appropriate.

The Secretary of State expects that where the unattached teacher is a special needs teacher, he or she will be awarded one or both of the special needs allowances where the circumstances are such that they would be awarded these allowances if they were in a school.

Relevant bodies have the discretion to pay teachers in charge of Pupil Referral Units (PRUs) on the teachers' pay spine. Teachers in charge of PRUs paid as Heads will be subject to the same conditions of employment as Heads.

Other unattached teachers who are paid as Heads or deputy heads will have their conditions of employment negotiated on a separate contractual basis.

Unqualified Teachers

Unqualified teachers are paid on a single ten-point scale. Relevant bodies must determine the starting point. Extra increments can be given up to the maximum when the relevant body considers this to be appropriate having regard to the qualifications and experience of the teacher or the responsibilities attached to the post.

Unqualified teachers are entitled to an increment if they have completed 26 weeks or more in aggregate within the previous 12 months.

The relevant body can withhold an annual increment if they consider the previous year's work to be unsatisfactory.

Can I earn any more than the laid-down scale of pay as an unqualified teacher?

The *School Teachers' Pay and Conditions Document* (STPCD) allows relevant bodies to make such additional allowances as they deem appropriate where they consider an unqualified teacher's salary to be inadequate in regard to the responsibilities, qualifications or experience relevant to his or her specialist area.

Appointments to a New School and Following a Break in Service

Teachers who have previously been in service in a maintained school must have their points entitlement formally assessed on appointment. This will determine the salary points of the new post (except where safeguarding applies or where their previous service entitles them to a higher points total). The calculation of the experience of a teacher returning after a break in service is in the annex of the STPCD. Teachers carry with them:

- any points they have been given for experience outside teaching
- their threshold enhancement.

Teachers moving to a new post do not carry with them:

- any cash safeguarding
- their London allowance.

What pay am I entitled to if I return to teaching after a break in service?

The rules are contained in the STCPD and guidance is given in the accompanying circular. A teacher returning to service always receives the highest version of whichever way their pay is calculated, according to the calculations in the annex to the Document.

Can I opt for a lower salary on returning to service?

The *School Teachers' Pay and Conditions Document* rules out the possibility of returning teachers taking a lower salary than their entitlement. It has been raised with, and so far rejected by, successive Secretaries of State.

Part-time Teachers

Qualified teachers in regular part-time service are paid a proportion of the remuneration that they would get if they were full-time. Their proportion of remuneration corresponds to the portion of the school week that the relevant body deems the teacher to be normally employed (excluding breaks between school sessions).

Teachers employed on a day-to-day or other short notice basis are paid in accordance with the STCPD provisions on a day basis, assuming that a full working year consists of 195 days. Periods of less than a day are calculated pro rata.

What happens to my salary when I have to move schools following a reorganisation?

In some circumstances teachers are entitled to retain existing salaries; in others they may do so at the discretion of the LEA or governing body.

If a teacher loses a post in a school which has been altered or significantly changed and is immediately employed in a post paid by the same authority, he or she is regarded as continuing in the same employment and hence keeps the same salary.

In other circumstances, eg when a teacher is redeployed between schools, the authority can decide whether such safeguarding should apply. However, the STPCD provides that the LEA should not "unreasonably refuse to exercise this discretion in favour of the teacher". In practice, LEAs either have an agreed cross-LEA policy or negotiate with the receiving school.

Responsibility points are safeguarded in the same way (unless they were temporary). Points for recruitment and retention are safeguarded only until the second 1 September following their award or confirmation. Points for excellence are safeguarded only until the 1 September following the award.

London Area Allowance

All teachers in the London area are entitled to this allowance. There are three rates relating to the inner, outer and fringe areas.

Acting Allowances

The relevant body is able to pay an acting allowance to a deputy (or classroom teacher) who has been acting as a Head for a prolonged period. A classroom teacher can also be paid an acting allowance when acting as a deputy head, or head of department, for a prolonged period.

Am I entitled to an extra allowance if I have been doing the job of my absent head of department for the past term? Would the situation be different if I was asked to carry out the deputy head's duties for a short while?

Schools should have a policy on this. LEAs usually have a policy for their schools, which governors must observe unless they have negotiated a different policy with staff. Schools cannot require staff to take on professional duties of senior staff but, if they do so, they should be prepared to negotiate an appropriate allowance.

The *School Teachers' Pay and Conditions of Employment* document only makes provision for acting allowances for those teachers temporarily carrying out the duties of a Head or deputy head. These are short-term appointments and are treated differently from the formally appointed acting heads, or deputy heads, who are appointed under the provisions of Schedule 14 of the **School Standards and Framework Act 1998** to fill a gap before a full-time head or deputy is appointed.

It is entirely a matter for the relevant body to determine whether to pay an acting allowance to a deputy acting as Head. If a teacher is asked to assume the duties of an absent Head or deputy and he or she agrees, then the relevant body has four weeks from the day on which the teacher assumes the temporary duties to determine whether to pay an allowance.

Acting allowance should be paid from, or backdated to, the time when the teacher assumed the extra tasks. A teacher who receives an acting allowance will be subject to the conditions of employment of that post for the time in which they hold it.

Payment for In-Service Training

Relevant bodies are able to pay all teachers, except Heads, for any INSET undertaken voluntarily at weekends or during school holidays.

Travelling Allowances

The *Burgundy Book* agreement commends to LEAs that, where teachers are requested by Heads or LEA officers to use their cars in order to facilitate the discharge of their duties, they should be paid an adequate mileage allowance to cover running costs, depreciation and insurance.

Teacher organisations and individual LEAs should negotiate the local rate. Independent schools and city technology colleges may negotiate separately with the staff but might bear in mind the local arrangements made by LEAs.

MATERNITY PAY AND MATERNITY LEAVE

A national scheme for statutory maternity pay and maternity leave is in existence giving maximum statutory rights.

As far as teachers in maintained schools are concerned, these were enhanced by agreements between teachers' unions and employers in 1985. These agreements are set out in the *Burgundy Book*, a revised edition of which was published in August 2000.

However, the **Employment Act 2002** has enhanced maternity provision. Maternity leave will be increased from 18 to 26 weeks, with a further entitlement to 26 weeks additional unpaid leave, as a basic right to women with 26 weeks' service at the 15th week before the expected date of the birth.

The main features of the local authority teacher scheme operative in September 2002 are as follows.

1. All female teachers, irrespective of length of service are entitled to remain on maternity leave for up to 18 weeks.
2. The absence cannot start earlier than the 11th week before the expected week of childbirth (EWC). The teacher cannot return to work earlier than two weeks after childbirth.
3. Female teachers with at least one year's continuous service with one or more LEA at the beginning of the 11th week before the EWC are entitled to additional leave for up to 29 weeks from the start of the week of the childbirth.
4. Payments to teachers with less than one year's continuous service are Statutory Maternity Pay (SMP) only. The entitlement of teachers with at least one year's continuous service is:
   - full pay for the first four weeks (offset by any SMP or Maternity Allowance)
   - $\frac{9}{10}$ of full pay for the next two weeks (offset as above)
   - half pay for the next 12 weeks; there are no deductions unless half pay and SMP added together exceed full pay
   - nil pay for the remaining absence.
5. The right to return, which is the right to return to the same job under the original contract of employment on terms and conditions no less

favourable than if she had not been absent. If the old job no longer exists because of redundancy, the teacher is entitled to be offered a suitable alternative vacancy where one exists.

6. Employers must be able to justify a decision to refuse to allow a new mother to return to work part-time.
7. The employer must be notified in writing at least 21 days before the day the teacher proposes to return, if the teacher intends to return early. If this notification is not given the employer can postpone the return for up to 21 days.
8. To enable the employer to calculate a proper date of return from additional maternity leave the teacher must give notice of the date of the birth.
9. If the teacher is unable to return to work because of ill health the normal sick pay procedures will apply.
10. A qualifying condition to occupational maternity pay is that the teacher returns to her job for at least 13 weeks (or part-time equivalent). Teachers with at least one year's continuous service are entitled to retain the first six weeks occupational maternity pay.

The **Employment Relations Act 1999** gives employees the right not to be victimised on the grounds of pregnancy, childbirth or maternity leave. Dismissal for a reason connected with pregnancy, childbirth or maternity leave is automatically unfair.

SICK PAY

On the first day of an illness, the teacher should inform the school of the nature and likely length of the illness. It is usual for teachers to send in work for their classes wherever possible. On day four of an illness, an employee should complete a self-certificate form and return it to the school.

Employers have the responsibility for paying statutory sick pay for periods of up to 28 weeks. LEAs (or schools) may have varying rules over the amounts to be paid depending on periods of service. According to the agreement set out in the *Burgundy Book*, a teacher absent through illness is entitled to receive, in any period of one-year, sick pay in accordance with the following scale:

- 1st year of service: full pay for 25 days and, after completing four calendar months' service, half pay for 50 working days
- 2nd year of service: full pay for 50 working days and half pay for 50 working days

- 3rd year: full pay for 75 working days, half pay for 75 working days
- 4th and successive years: full pay for 100 working days and half pay for 100 working days.

On returning to work after a prolonged illness, an employee should bring a medical certificate to say he or she is fit for work.

EQUAL PAY

The **Equal Pay Act 1970** (as amended) provides for equal pay between men and women.

Any employee can compare himself or herself with a comparator in one of three ways:

- employment is "like work" with the comparator
- employment is for work rated as equivalent
- employment is for work of equal value.

The comparisons can be made between employees of the same employer, even if they work at different establishments. This means that a teacher could compare himself or herself with a teacher at another LEA school, if the LEA is the employer of both.

What does "like work" mean?

If a woman is employed in "like", if not equivalent, work as a man, and is less favourably treated in contractual terms than the man, then the woman's contract should be modified to equate with the man's.

What is "work rated as equivalent"?

An Employment Tribunal would consider all the surrounding facts and determine whether the work was equivalent. Again, if a woman was receiving less money than a man for equivalent work, the Tribunal could order that her contract be changed.

The jobs must be compared objectively and analytically according to the demands made on the employees, judged under a non-discriminatory job evaluation.

In *Hanlon v Kirklees M.B.C* (1990), a female teacher on a standard scale salary successfully contended that she should be paid an incentive allowance based on a comparison with specified male colleagues.

An independent expert compared the job specifications and responsibilities of the male assistant heads of Art, English and Mathematics. The skills, judgment, control of others, responsibility for resources, effort and working environment of each was assessed. The conclusion was that the female teacher's post was not of equal value in one case, was greater in another and at least of equal value in the third. The value of the post was upgraded and back pay for some three years was agreed.

What is "work of equal value"?

Where a woman (or man) is employed on work which does not fall under the two headings above, but which is of equal value in terms of the demands made on her (or him) as that of a person of the opposite gender in the same employment, then a Tribunal can change the contract to ensure equal pay. The employer may prove that the difference is genuinely due to a material factor other than a difference in sex. For example, one employee may have agreed to undertake additional duties.

In *Ward v Davis and Cheshire C.C.*, a sole Drama teacher in a school was paid on the standard scale. She claimed that she should be paid the same B allowance as the head of Music. The Tribunal held that, even though the Music teacher was responsible for two other teachers, the essence of the jobs was such that they were of equal value.

However, it was shown by the school that the recruitment of Music teachers was difficult at the time of the employment of the head of Music and so there was a rationale for paying him more. This criterion is one set out in the *School Teachers' Pay and Conditions Document* and the LEA produced national statistics to demonstrate the points.

Does the comparator have to teach in the same school as the claimant?

It is usual for a female teacher to choose a male comparator in the same school (or vice versa) but it is not absolutely necessary. If an employee alleges unlawful gender discrimination of any kind and the comparator is not in the same workplace, the claimant has to show that the employers were "associated" within the meaning of s.1 of the **Equal Pay Act 1970**.

In a recent school case in Scotland, *South Ayrshire Council v Morton* (2000), a court was persuaded to allow comparison between the pay of teachers in two separate local authorities. The court could see that there was a sufficient connection in a loose and non-technical sense between the two employers. An important consideration was the existence of national pay scales and the fact that education is a service provided generally across Scotland. This created a reasonable basis for comparison.

INCOME TAX

Teachers, like any other employees, are subject to the self-assessment of income tax scheme.

Tax returns have to be completed and returned. Employers will also provide a P11D statement of the expenses and benefits in kind allowed to them during the year in question.

The financial deadline for receipt of tax returns is 31 January. Anyone who has not paid tax due by the end of February of the following year will be automatically surcharged.

Records will normally be retained for 22 months from the end of the tax year. Some documents may have to be kept for longer periods.

Further information is available in the Inland Revenue booklet SA/BK4 *Self-Assessment: A General Guide to Keeping Records.*

Some records that have to be kept are:

- Form P60 — the employer's certificate giving details of employees' pay and tax deducted
- Form P45 — certificates from former employers
- Form P160 (Part 1A) — a form from an employer when an employee retires or goes onto a pension paid by the employer
- details of any other taxable receipts and benefits not included in the above records (for teachers, some travel claims will fall under this heading; Booklet 480 *Expenses and Benefits: A Tax Guide* gives further guidance).

PAYE

Teachers are normally part of PAYE systems and will receive pay slips each month detailing amounts paid and deducted.

TEACHERS' PENSIONS

Teachers normally belong to the Teachers' Superannuation Scheme, a contributory scheme run by the agency, Teachers' Pensions. A booklet *Your Pension: A Guide to Teachers' Superannuation* is available from Teachers' Pensions at Mowden Hall, Darlington, County Durham DL3 9EE.

Teachers, at maintained or independent schools that are in the Teacher's Superannuation Scheme, can be members of the scheme. Part-time teachers can elect to have their service treated as pensionable. Form 477 PEN, included in *Leaflet 476,* is used to make the election.

Can I opt out of the Teachers' Superannuation Scheme?

Teachers have the right to opt out of the Teachers' Superannuation Scheme and to take out their own Personal Pension Plan. To do this, *Form PEN TR 263* has to be completed. *Leaflet 735: A Guide for Early Leavers* gives further advice.

Past Added Years

A teacher can buy in, at full cost, past years which would not otherwise count for benefits. The cost depends on age and salary. Payment can be by lump sum, by instalments or deductions from salary.

Family Benefits

Within the Teachers' Pension Scheme (TPS) there is provision for "family benefits" based on all service from 1 April 1972 for men and from 6 April 1988 for women, unless an election was made within six months to purchase service prior to those dates.

CONTRIBUTIONS

A teacher pays 6.0% of their salary, deducted monthly, and the employer pays 7.25% of the salary. The pension package, therefore, is 13.25% of the salary. In addition teacher contributions attract income tax relief.

A teacher can make extra contributions to provide extra pension by:

- buying in for past added years of service, after the age of 20, that are not counted as pensionable service
- paying Additional Voluntary Contributions (AVCs) to a scheme provided by the Prudential (see below)
- paying into schemes provided by other insurance companies called free-standing AVCs.

Inland revenue regulations impose a limit of 15% of the salary on contributions to pension funds. Thus, teachers could elect to pay a further 9% of their salary.

Additional Voluntary Contributions

The Additional Voluntary Contribution (AVC) is a scheme which invests AVCs in stocks and shares. Prudential was the company chosen by the DfES, local authorities and the teachers' organisations to run this scheme. AVCs can be used to increase pensions, a dependant's pension or the lump sum death grant; or a combination of these.

A teacher can also pay an AVC into a personal policy with an insurance company. This is known as a "freestanding" AVC.

Teachers contemplating making additional contributions should seek independent financial advice. Unions can point teachers in the direction of professional help.

RETIREMENT

Full pension entitlement can be drawn at 60 years of age but a teacher can remain in service to 65 and even after that, if agreed with employers, until the maximum of 70 years.

The maximum service for pension purposes is 45 years. Service in excess of this does not count but the pension and lump sum continues to be based on the "average salary".

Benefits are paid at the age of 60 or over on application to Teachers' Pensions using Form 14 PEN obtainable from the employer.

Applications should be made some four months before retirement.

Calculation of Pension

There are two kinds of benefit:

- an annual pension
- a tax-free lump sum.

The annual pension is calculated at 1/80 of the "average salary" for all years and days of reckonable service. An "average salary" is the best 365 days' salary earned in the last 1095 days of reckonable service.

The one-off lump sum is calculated at 3/80 of the "average salary" for all years and days of reckonable service.

Teachers' pensions are index-linked based on rises in the retail price index. Increases become payable in April annually, but do not normally apply to teachers who retire before 55.

There are arrangements for transferring pension benefits from one scheme to another. Transfer to the teachers' scheme must be done within one year of entering pensionable teaching service.

Infirmity Pension

An infirmity pension is payable to a teacher before the age of 60 who has become incapable through infirmity of mind or body of serving efficiently as a teacher.

The calculation is the same as the pension and lump sum for premature retirement, but can be enhanced by extra service to compensate for early retirement. *Leaflet 198: Infirmity Pensions: A Guide* gives details.

Application is made by completing *Form 18 PEN*. A medical examination is necessary.

Early Retirement

A teacher over 50 where service has been terminated through redundancy, or in the efficient discharge of the employer's functions, can receive pension benefits. The teacher's application has to be supported by an employer's certification of one of these two reasons.

Pensions are calculated in the normal way. There is no automatic enhancement as there is with infirmity pensions but employers may enhance the teacher's service as compensation for having to retire early. *Leaflet 144: Agreed Premature Retirement Benefit* gives further details. The application is via *Form 14PR PEN*.

A teacher over 55 can now apply for premature retirement with an actuarially reduced pension. Details can be obtained from Teachers' Pensions and the application form is *Form 14ARB* (April 2000).

INSURANCE

Teachers are covered in their work by their employer's policies whether the work is in school or on outside activities approved by the school. Claims made against teachers for negligence and accidents to teachers are all included.

Damage to, or loss of, personal property may not be covered by an LEA or school. Teachers should check this and determine whether to carry their own insurance. Teachers' unions often offer cover as an automatic membership benefit.

For residential visits and visits abroad, it is usual to take out holiday-type insurance covering all members of the party including pupils.

Motor Insurance

Teachers should check that their own car insurance covers them for "business use". It is advisable to have full comprehensive insurance.

Should a teacher allow a pupil to drive other students in his or her car?

Schools should have a policy on this. Generally, such a practice should be discouraged but sometimes sixth formers may want to visit a theatre or an art gallery, etc and a large party led by a teacher is impossible or impracticable.

It is up to the Head, not the teacher, to make the decision. The Head is likely, if minded to allow the party to travel in a student's car, to check the insurance and MOT certificate, ensure that the car's owners have given permission and the students' parents have also been informed and given permission.

CHAPTER 4

THE TEACHER'S JOB

CONDITIONS OF EMPLOYMENT

The Conditions of Employment of Heads, deputy heads and teachers are contained in the *School Teachers' Pay and Conditions Document* (STPCD).

Heads

Heads must carry out their duties in accordance with the provision of Education Acts and any orders and regulations, the Articles of Government and the LEA's local management scheme (LMS).

The Head must also follow rules, regulations and policies set out by the governing body.

The Head is then responsible for the internal organisation, management and control of the school and must consult variously with governing bodies, LEA, staff and parents.

It is expected that in the near future teachers wishing to apply for their first headship will need to have passed the National Professional Qualification for Headship (NPQH).

Deputy Heads

Deputy heads have the same professional duties as classroom teachers (see below). They are also required to play a major role in formulating the aims and objectives of the school and in management tasks delegated by the Head. When the Head is absent, the deputy head undertakes the full range of professional duties of the Head.

Teachers Other than Heads or Deputy Heads

Classroom teachers are required to work under the reasonable direction of the Head.

Subject Heads

The generic conditions of employment for subject heads are the same as for all classroom teachers, but by virtue of their position they will have additional specific responsibilities.

The recommended National Standards for subject leaders are divided into five parts.

1. The core purpose of subject leadership.
2. The key outcomes of subject leadership.
3. Professional knowledge and understanding.
4. Skills and attributes.
5. The key areas of subject leadership.

There is a related set of standards for Special Education Needs (SEN) Co-ordinators.

Further information about the National Standards can be found on the DfES website: *www.dfes.gov.uk/teachers/professional_development*.

TEACHERS' PROFESSIONAL DUTIES

Teachers' professional duties, which they have to carry out within the reasonable discretion of the Head, are set out in Part XI of the STPCD. Any teacher teaching in the school, even if teaching at other schools as well, comes under the reasonable direction of the Head while in that school.

Teaching Duties

Teaching duties are planning and preparing courses and lessons, teaching pupils according to their educational needs, including the setting and marking of work, assessing, recording and reporting on the development, progress and attainment of pupils.

These duties are at the heart of a teacher's professional responsibilities.

Teachers are expected to assist the Head in meeting the statutory duty to provide the National Curriculum as laid down and any other provisions in the governors' curriculum policy.

How do teachers know what to teach?

Maintained schools have to include the subjects of the National Curriculum in the programmes of study of all pupils of statutory school age "for a reasonable time". Schools also have to include Religious Education for all pupils in the school whose parents have not opted them out.

The content of the National Curriculum is set out in Orders and is contained in a document which all schools possess.

The National Curriculum is not expected to take up all the school time available. Other subjects/experiences can be included in the school's full programme.

Links with External Agencies

Teachers normally volunteer to be involved with outside bodies, but they can be directed to do so by the Head so long as this is part of "directed time" and is a reasonable directive in the circumstances.

Liaison with education welfare officers, the careers service, school psychologists, school medical service, etc is an obvious obligation. Usually it is nominated members of staff who are responsible for this. Liaison with other bodies, such as parents' associations, Chambers of Commerce, higher education institutions and further education colleges is also a vital part of school life and service to the pupils. Any direction to co-operate with these bodies is entirely reasonable so long as it follows due consultation and agreement. It is rare for any problem to arise about this particular duty, although various problems may arise in the exercise of it.

Teachers should have the right to refuse a request to be visited by the media while at work, eg local newspaper reporter, film crew, even if the request comes from the Head or another more senior member of staff.

Are schools obliged to co-operate with the police?

Provisions were made in the **Education (No.2) Act 1986** designed to strengthen schools' relationships with the police. Governors and Heads of county, controlled and maintained special schools have a duty under s.18 to have regard to any representations about curriculum matters made by a local chief police officer.

Police officers have no right of access to the classroom but any representation made by or on behalf of the local chief police officer (usually the Chief Constable or nominee) must be considered by a governing body and any failure to do so could be questioned in the courts. Teachers could be involved in any results of the co-operation between police and the governors and Head.

In most areas, arrangements exist for police and school liaison on a regular basis.

Cover Arrangements

The teachers' duties in respect of cover are set out in the STPCD and explained in the accompanying circular.

Teachers, including deputy heads, are obliged to cover for absent staff within certain limits. Teachers are not required to cover for a teacher who is absent for three or more consecutive days or where the three-day absence of the teacher was known to the school for two or more working days before the absence commenced.

This does not apply if the school has "exhausted all reasonable means of providing supply cover without success".

Equally, it does not apply to supply teachers or part-time teachers engaged for up to 75% of the pupil week to carry out specified duties.

Normally, schools operate an equitable rota system for cover and have, along with LEAs, a list of qualified persons willing to cover for absent staff.

In 2001, the Government made a concession to teachers regarding staff cover. Teachers may now aggregate the time spent on covering for absent staff beyond the statutory requirement, and take time off equal to that amount.

Administration

Teachers have a duty to participate in administrative and organisational tasks including management of support personnel and equipment and materials, attending assemblies, registering attendance of pupils and supervising pupils before, during or after school sessions.

Do I have to attend morning assembly?

A teacher is obliged to be present at morning assembly, but not for the collective worship element. It is usual for amicable agreements to be reached with the Head over the proper approach to this.

Registration

Teachers have a duty to register the pupils in their forms or tutor groups at the beginning of the morning and afternoon sessions of the school day as directed by the Head. Schools can decide the timing of afternoon registration. They have an obligation to complete the register as instructed and to provide the statistics required by the school. Registers are legal documents and must be looked after.

Keeping Records

As part of their duty of care, teachers keep records on pupils' progress, of discussions between them, of aspirations and problems. Much of this information finds its way into periodic reports.

Pupil records

Teachers must keep a curricular record for each pupil, covering their academic achievements, other skills and abilities and general progress in the school. This must be updated every year. Schools may also ask teachers to keep other records which are not actually required by law.

Apart from certain confidential information, parents and pupils over 18 can have access to their records.

Information about pupils with special educational needs comes under other regulations.

National record of achievement

The National Record of Achievement (NRA) was launched in 1991 and is now used in most schools. It is a format for recording a summary of pupils' educational achievements and consists of a number of standard sheets where the following information can be recorded:

- personal details
- personal statement
- school achievements
- attendance rate
- qualifications and credits
- achievements and experiences

- employment history
- individual action plan.

The NRA is intended to be used throughout a person's life to record their progress and achievement. The NRA is due to be replaced by the "Progress File" when trials have been completed.

Who can see these records?

Schools have to make a good deal of information about the school in general and pupils' achievements available to members of the public. Teachers have a duty to supply such information as is necessary for this. Information about individual pupils, however, can only be shown to parents or carers, not to the public.

The information is usually passed on as the child progresses so that other teachers can be informed.

Are teachers obliged to provide reports to parents?

Heads have to ensure that a written report is sent at least annually to parents. If only one report is sent, it must contain specified minimum information laid down in the current Individual Pupils' Achievements Information Regulations. This includes particulars of achievements, general progress, results of examinations, attendance record and some comparative information.

It is a teacher's duty to participate in providing relevant information under arrangements made by the Head. It is usual for these arrangements to have been discussed by staff at some stage, and, therefore, have a measure of agreement.

The format of the reports is up to the school so long as it is consistent with the supply of minimum information.

Are there different arrangements for school leavers?

If a pupil leaves to go to another school, the Head has to provide the receiving school with a report. All leavers are entitled to their own report on their school achievements, which must include a set format taken from the NRA.

The form has to be signed and dated by a teacher who knows the child. The pupil can also sign.

The filling-in of this record does not preclude an even fuller report being provided.

Can parents see the records of their child?

All schools must have arrangements for keeping and updating individual records of progress. A pupil's record must be disclosed free of charge to parents (and pupil, if over 16) and any institution to which the pupil transfers.

If a pupil's reference for a job or university application is kept semi-permanently on a computer, then parents and pupils have a right to see them. If they are not on computer, they can remain confidential if the school so wishes. In the future, this may cease to be the case.

Attending Meetings

Teachers have a duty to participate in meetings relating to the curriculum administration or organisation, including pastoral arrangements.

The amount of time spent in such meetings should be reflected in the *time-budget* of the statutory 1265 hours spread over 195 days.

It is not sufficient for a teacher simply to attend such meetings. The section specifically refers to "participating in". It is not usually a problem for teachers to take part in discussions about their working role and tasks!

Managing Other Staff

Teachers are required to contribute to the selection and progressional development of other staff, including the induction and assessment of new teachers, and to the management of work of other teachers.

They are also obliged to participate in the management of activities relating to the curriculum, organisation and pastoral functions.

Heads of department and subjects have a clear duty to exercise managerial functions.

The rules concerning selection and appointment are set out in the chapter on *Teachers' Conditions of Service*.

Qualified teacher status (QTS) can be granted to students who have successfully completed initial teacher training (ITT) in an LEA maintained school. Circulars 9/92 and 14/93 set out specified criteria although the curriculum for teacher training is under review.

Am I obliged to take part in the induction of new teachers?

The responsibility for planning and management of Initial Teacher Training is shared by the receiving school and higher education institutions (HEI) partner.

Teachers at the school are obliged to participate in these schemes as far as what is requested of them lies within their normal managerial responsibilities. For many years, schools have supervised students on teaching practice and well established procedures should be in place. Further unreasonable demands should not be made without the member of staff volunteering or agreeing to undertake them.

Most teachers are very willing to help to inaugurate young staff into the mysteries of the profession. It is only when too much is asked of them that questions are raised.

It is also possible for teachers to be paid for extra duties associated with Initial Teacher Training (see Chapter 3, page 80)

THE DUTY OF CARE

Health and Safety

All school authorities have both statutory and common law duties to ensure that schools are safe and healthy places for employees and pupils. If schools fail in this, they could be sued for damages in a civil court or prosecuted in a criminal court. The Health and Safety Executive, the Government's enforcing agency, takes a close interest in schools.

LEAs must have general health and safety policies and so must all school governing bodies. The **Health and Safety at Work, etc Act 1974** and accompanying regulations lay on all employers a duty to take care of health, safety and welfare of all who work in the school or who visit it.

The requirements for LEAs is to keep school healthy and safe "so far as is reasonably practicable". This is not as loose as it appears since a plethora of regulations initiated by European Commission Directives have laid precise duties on employers and employees in many circumstances.

What are employees' duties?

All those involved in running a school must do everything to make the environment safe and healthy. Employees must take reasonable care for their own health and safety and for the health and safety of others at work. Detailed policies must be in place and known to all employees in the school. Each school should have a health and safety representative. Most also have health and safety committees. At the request of at least two safety representatives, the employer must establish a safety committee. It is usual for larger primary school and secondary schools to have a safety committee.

Regular risk assessments must be initiated by the Head and problems put to right.

Employees should report any problems or defects to the health and safety representative or to the person indicated in the school policy.

What constitutes "reasonably practicable"?

What is "reasonably practicable" depends of the facts of each case. If an employee is so uncaring and reckless that he or she exposes himself or herself or others to needless danger, then that employee will be guilty of an offence. However, if employees show a proper regard for their own and others' health and safety, they would not be negligent or criminally liable if something went wrong. It is important, therefore, not to ignore defective equipment or unsafe parts of the premises. It is everyones duty to report these.

We come back to notions of thoughtfulness, prudence and common sense.

When is an accident an accident and when is it negligence?

Accidents are common in schools. When they happen it should be considered whether anything could have been done to prevent them. Being concerned and conscience-stricken is different from being legally liable.

Everyone feels a little "responsible" when an accident happens, but for someone to be legally liable for damages, the law requires the injured party to show that, on balance of probability, the teacher was "negligent", ie did do something that there was an obligation not to or vice versa.

There does not have to be an *intention* to hurt anybody. The guide used by the court is "would a reasonable person have acted the same way in similar circumstances?"

In 1954, Mr Justice McNair summed up the teacher's dilemma succinctly when he said that a balance must be found between meticulously supervising pupils every moment they are at school and encouraging "sturdy independence" as they grow up.

In Loco Parentis

The Latin phrase *in loco parentis* means "in place of the parent" and is a notion that pervades everything a teacher does for, with and on behalf of the pupils he or she is looking after. It may be considered a strange concept, as few parents are likely to have 30 children at one time to look after, and none at all exchange this 30 for another 30 at regular intervals!

However, the phrase points in its cryptic way to the prime concern of a teacher, now set down in statutory conditions of employment — the "well-being of pupils" and their general progress.

The characteristics a teacher must display are those of a caring, prudent parent who might find themselves in a school context. It is probably a higher than average responsibility since teachers are actually trained professionals. This is particularly so in specialist areas such as PE, technology and science and for activities outside school (see page 134). The increase in litigation when accidents happen has understandably made teachers more wary about all activities involving higher levels of risk.

There has been a move in court judgements towards defining the duty of care less in comparison with the notion of "a parent", and more in terms of what a "reasonable and responsible" teacher might be expected to do in the circumstances.

Is there a limit to the comparison with a parent?

Like a parent, a teacher can praise and admonish and keep a child indoors (detention) but, unlike a parent, no teacher may now hit a child, not even gently (see below). Like a parent, a teacher must always be mindful of the pupil's safety and welfare.

What should I do if I am not sure about what I am doing?

By and large all those who have made teaching their career have relatively little trouble with the enormity of the task. However, for all of us there are moments of doubt and self-questioning. Bear in mind at all times the question "if I were a parent of one of these children, would I consider what I was doing, or contemplating doing, to be reasonable and prudent in the circumstances?" The answers will take into account:

- the nature of the task
- any hazards that could reasonably be anticipated; for activities in schools involving unusual or additional risks there are now standard risk assessment procedures
- the age, ability and aptitude of the children
- the environment in which the task is to take place
- any LEA or school procedures that have to be followed.

The law requires a teacher as a highly trained professional not to be careless or, at worst, reckless. If it can be shown that a teacher has acted after due thoughtfulness, it is extremely unlikely that any mishap will occur and, if it does, that the teacher would be negligent.

How do teachers know that they are reaching the standard?

The standard of care according to the Court in *Lyes v Middlesex C.C.* (1962) is of a reasonably prudent parent judged not in the context of his or her own home but in the context of a school, ie a person displaying the responsible, mental qualities of a prudent parent in the circumstances of school life.

Heads and governing bodies (and LEAs) have responsibilities to ensure that policies are in place, assessment of risks are carried out regularly, safe systems of supervision are in place and staff are properly trained to operate these systems effectively.

Teachers have a duty to assist the Head in this task, and should carry out any reasonable directions and follow any guidelines issued. Where a teacher is called upon to make a decision on a safety matter he or she will not be expected to make one particular judgement, but will be expected to have chosen a course of action that is "within a range of reasonable responses".

Educational Visits

Health and safety considerations on school visits are in essence no different from those in school. The difference is mainly that the environment is unfamiliar, and the activities often beyond the teacher's normal range. Therefore, more careful consideration has to be given to assessing beforehand any risks likely to attend the visit, and to make plans to manage and minimise them. This is normally a formal process of determining the likely risks, looking at what is already in place to combat these and considering what extra provision needs to be made. There is also a requirement to do continuous risk assessment as the visit progresses. But teachers do this all the time in the classroom, and should not feel that there is some particular skill involved. Teachers leading groups on visits simply have to remain alert to the changing environment and activities as the visit progresses, and consider whether any extra precautionary action needs to be taken at any point. It is a fact that teachers have done this brilliantly for many years, so that thousands of school visits are run extremely safely every year.

Activities Outside School and School Visits

Thousands of pupil visits take place each year, to places close to the school and much further afield. Very few accidents happen, due to the care taken over the efficient organisation and careful control of the visits.

However, teachers are naturally concerned over the legal and insurance aspects. All LEAs and schools should have policies, procedures and guidelines covering all types of activity. These should be reviewed regularly.

Teachers organising a school visit must follow the school's policies and procedures. In particular an organiser should check:

- what permission is required
- ratio of staff to pupils allowed
- who should accompany the group
- what forms have to be completed
- equipment and clothing necessary for the activities
- that rules and routines are made known to all the party
- that travel arrangements and accommodation are checked for safety
- that codes of practice are known, eg mountain code, highway code, country code
- insurance arrangements
- information to be given to parents
- any medical, allergy or diet problems in the group
- arrangements for any children with special needs
- emergency arrangements
- collection of money procedure
- minibus regulations
- rabies regulations (for visits abroad); every member of the party must be aware of the rabies regulations and organisers must complete a "*Danger from Rabies*" form.

The DfES good practice guide *Health and Safety of Pupils on Educational Visits* (HASPEV) 1998 sets out principles of good practice for Heads, teachers and governors .

Three supplementary guides to HASPEV 1998 were published in 2002: Standards for LEAs in *Overseeing Educational Visits, Standards for Adventure* and *A Handbook for Group Leaders*.

Adventurous activities

Activities in adventure centres are now covered by legislation and regulations. Strict codes cover the licensing of the centre, the qualifications of staff, the centre's safety and emergency policies, insurance arrangements and the accommodation.

The Adventure Activities Licensing Authority is at Tourism Quality Services, 17 Lambourne Crescent, Llanishen, Cardiff CF4 5GG (tel: 029 2075 5715).

Nevertheless, each school has a duty to check that the required safety precautions are in place in each centre used. Circular 22/94 *Safety in Outdoor Activity Centres* gives detailed guidance and lists further documents.

> *What should I do if I do not like what the expert is doing with any group?*
> The school group leader hands over the control of the activities of the group to any trained expert engaged for that purpose, eg a ski or canoe instructor or mountain leader. However, the school leader still retains overall control. A teacher who is concerned about the safety of the group should step in and take over control. A group leader should not, however, initiate activities without an expert's approval. In other words, at all times the most safe course should be followed.

Casual activities outside school

Teachers often take pupils out of school during a lesson for, say, a traffic survey or visit to a local farm or factory.

It is important not to neglect the legal responsibility and safety aspects. Schools should have a policy on such activities. Permission should be obtained and the whereabouts of the group known. Many schools now have mobile telephones for the use of the teacher on these occasions.

Indemnity forms

Some schools ask parents to sign forms indemnifying the school and teachers-in-charge against any claims arising from any cause. Such forms do not protect teachers from being sued for any negligence which causes death or personal injury. Parents cannot be required to sign away their rights.

A slightly different type of indemnity form informs the parent of the nature of the visit and is worded in such a way as to indemnify school or teacher against any loss that might be caused by the actions of the pupil (eg if a pupil causes damage on a visit which the teacher pays for).

Emergencies

In an emergency, eg an accident on a school visit, a teacher may have to act as though he or she was the parent (*in loco parentis*) and give permission for a child to receive emergency treatment, including medicines and blood transfusions.

It is usual for parents to have given permission on the school visit form, but the provisions of the **Children Act 1989** allow decisions to be taken by those who have care of a child.

A teacher in these circumstances has a duty to use his or her judgment as to the action that is in the best interests of the child.

Volunteers

Parents often volunteer to help in school — with libraries, reading schemes, performing arts and sporting activities, for example.

All volunteers are subject to the requirement to disclose any convictions, etc and to seek a declaration through the Criminal Records Bureau in the same way that teachers have to.

A teacher in charge should ensure that such helpers are familiar with the activity and know what is expected of them. If in charge of a game, they must know the rules and be able to enforce them.

In some situations, eg swimming or other dangerous pursuits, a volunteer should not be left alone. It ought to be rare for a volunteer to be left entirely alone since they are there by definition to "help" and not take over the teaching.

So long as the volunteer is supervised and is acting within the remit given, and not doing something outside that remit, the local authority's or school's insurance policies will cover them and the supervisory teacher.

The Duty of Care of Specialist Teachers

Physical education

Clearly a greater chance of accidents happening exists in gyms and on playing fields. Only qualified PE teachers trained in the use of specialist equipment should be allowed to use that equipment. Equally, only teachers who know how certain potentially dangerous games should be played (eg hockey or rugby football) should supervise these games.

Trained PE teachers will know the rules concerning binding in the front row of rugby football scrums or the dangers of the "Fosbury flop" in high-jumping, and other such restrictions.

For some activities, such as trampolining, extra training is given to ensure that teachers are conversant with safety procedures.

How do I know whether my procedures are safe?

Emphasised in the training of PE teachers is the paramount concern for safety. Trained teachers will have dealt with all normal circumstances. Sometimes, however, the circumstances in a particular school may be different from anything previously experienced.

The teacher can either change the practice or rely on the fact that the school's approved practices have stood it in good stead over a period of time.

For example, in the leading case of *Wright v Cheshire* C.C. (1952), a class in a gym was involved in four different exercises in different parts of the gym. One boy fell when attempting to vault while the teacher was dealing with one of the other groups. The court held that the supervision at the time accorded with the normal, accepted practice in the school and had been safely used for many years.

On the other hand, in another case, *Gibbs v Barking Corporation* (1936), when a boy also fell while vaulting without a competent supporter or "stand by" at the side of the horse, the teacher was held to be negligent.

As in all other cases, a PE teacher has to ask himself or herself, "could I as a competent PE teacher have reasonably foreseen the set of concurrent circumstances which caused this accident?" All teachers have to think ahead and anticipate possible risks while at the same time allowing youngsters the opportunity to grow to "sturdy independence".

It is unlikely that any teacher would echo the sentiment of the judge in *Suckling v Essex* C.C.(1955) who said, "it is better a boy should break his neck than allow other people to break his spirit". However, teachers have a duty to face children with acceptable challenges, doing so in a way that is as safe as is reasonably practicable.

Can I insist on pupils doing PE in bare feet if they have forgotten their plimsolls?

If it is acceptable to the school, then it is probably safe to allow a child to do some activities in bare feet. Clearly it would be inappropriate where the activity is likely to harm the underside of the foot.

It is probably not acceptable, however, for pupils to do any PE activity in stockinged feet. It has been held that the risks of slipping and being injured are greater when wearing socks than when in plimsolls or bare feet.

Does a PE teacher have to accept a note from a parent excusing a child from PE?

Although many teachers at times find some excuse notes suspicious, short of checking every time with parents, the best advice is to accept them. A check could be made at times through the child's form tutor to ensure that the school is not being taken for a ride.

The reason why parents' excuse notes should be taken seriously was highlighted in *Moore v Hampshire C.C.* in 1982. A mother had written to the school explicitly stating that because of a congenital defect, her daughter should not do any PE. The mother also talked to the Head and the decision was noted in the girl's records. One day, the girl turned up with PE shorts and expressed her keenness to join in the lessons. She persuaded the PE teacher to let her take part. She injured her ankle and the parents sued for damages. The Court of Appeal said that the teacher should first of all have checked with the parent and secondly should have ensured that the girl was given closer attention and more positive instructions on joining the class. "It was a case without defence," the judge said.

Can parents or other unqualified persons be allowed to referee or supervise games?

Schools should have a policy on this. There is nothing intrinsically wrong in non-PE trained persons refereeing or supervising games. After all, most amateur referees are from other walks of life. The important aspect is whether they understand the rules and regulations and know when play is unsafe.

In *Nolan v Smolden* (1996), a referee of a rugby match, involving under 18 year olds which took place outside normal school hours, was found to have breached the duty of care that he owed to a 17 year old who was severely injured during the game. He was adjudged to have failed to apply the particular rules that are applicable to under 18s matches.

An even higher standard is likely to be required in school games. A check should be made of every non-PE department referee or coach to ensure that they know what they are doing. They should also be properly briefed by PE department staff, preferably the head of PE or the person best qualified in that pursuit.

Should a teacher take part in games with school children?

This depends very much on the particular game and the age and aptitude of the pupils. Teachers should not now take part in physical contact games, except to demonstrate for a short while a particular technique — and even here the teacher should avoid physical contact as far as possible.

In *Affutu Nartoy v Clarke (1984)*, a teacher played on one side in a game of rugby between 15 year olds. He chased after a high kick and high tackled the boy who caught the ball. The boy received a serious back injury. The Court held that the teacher was negligent because he took no account of his advantage in height, weight, strength, skill and experience putting young children at risk if he came into physical contact with them. It would not have been wrong to put himself in one team in order to demonstrate normal contact skills but he should have foreseen the consequences of his taking part vigorously in the game.

Teachers have to bear in mind the difference between their own physical growth and the pupils' and any participation should bear this in mind. It is particularly important to remember this in end-of-term "jolly" matches between staff and pupils.

Games between school teams and adult teams are now either forbidden or are strictly controlled by the regulations of some governing bodies of sports, notably rugby football.

Dangerous places

In addition to gyms and sports fields, other parts of a school have a higher propensity for danger than normal. Workshops and science laboratories clearly have this potential.

Each department should have health and safety booklets and many teachers will have attended safety courses. All newly qualified teachers of Science, for example, should attend such a course within their first year. At the very least, the head of department should ensure that safety and emergency procedures are known and understood by all staff. The review of health and safety in more dangerous places should be part of a regular process undertaken by relevant staff and possibly governors (see page 123).

What should I do if I consider aspects of my lesson to be dangerous?

Where an element of danger might be present in a lesson, a teacher should warn the whole class of the danger and instruct them in the conduct and procedures required.

In *Crouch v Essex C.C.* (1966), a Chemistry teacher constantly warned his class of the danger of playing about with chemicals. During the course of one lesson, a girl squirted liquid concentrated caustic soda into a boy's eyes. He claimed negligence on the part of the teacher.

The judge held that there was evidence of horseplay in the lesson but not such as to create foreseeable danger. Proper warnings had been given and all the class knew of the dangers. The girl's act was "little short of lunatic" and could not have been foreseen by the teacher.

On the other hand, in *Norman v ILEA* (1974), it was held that a teacher had not given a graphic enough warning about the dangers of sulphuric acid which might have prevented a boy from squirting it at another boy. The acids were not clearly labelled and the class had been led to believe that they would be. This, coupled with the lack of specific oral warning, meant that the high standard demanded had not been met.

The same high standard applies to Craft teachers, too. Rules should be made and enforced concerning, for example, long hair and jewellery, which might get caught in machinery.

Machinery in Home Economics/Food Technology can also be dangerous. In *Fryer v Selford Corporation* (1937), an 11-year-old girl was injured when her gown caught fire. The question of appropriate clothing and overalls is one that should be considered and ruled on by each head of department and strictly adhered to by teachers of those subjects.

Guidance and Advice to Pupils

Teachers are required to provide guidance and advice to pupils on educational and social matters and on future education and careers. They are also required to make relevant records and reports.

In the daily round of teaching, teachers do not usually find much difficulty in this duty of guiding and advising pupils or in exercising their professional discretion in writing reports and keeping relevant records.

The curriculum that teachers teach stems from the exercise of the governing body's duties to determine their secular curriculum policies and to keep them under review. The Head's job is to organise the curriculum and to ensure it is followed in the school. LEAs also have a duty to determine their policy in respect of their schools, which the governors may modify but not change completely.

Promoting Pupils' Progress

The supervision of children in teachers' care goes beyond the legal and professional duty to teach them effectively each according to his or her abilities. There is an additional legal and moral duty to see that they come to no harm. It is called "the duty of care".

Since teachers are acting *in loco parentis* while pupils are at school or elsewhere when supervised by teachers, the standard by which this duty is measured is that of "a reasonably prudent parent".

Assessment and Reports

Teachers are obliged to provide or contribute to oral and written assessments, reports and references relating to individual pupils and groups of pupils.

Teachers are obliged to report to Heads, heads of departments and parents in accordance with the school's practice. This includes discussing a pupil's progress with parents on formal parents' evenings or on informal occasions. A time allowance for these activities should be made by the school within the statutory directed time.

Assessments

Schools must report National Curriculum assessment results to parents and publish these in prospectuses and annual reports. The legal requirements for pupils are:

- *7 year olds*: results of National Curriculum tasks and/or tests in reading, writing, spelling and Mathematics and separate teacher assessments in English, Mathematics and Science
- *11 year olds*: results of teacher assessments and National Curriculum tests in English, Mathematics and Science
- *14 year olds*: results of teacher assessments in all the National Curriculum subjects and National Curriculum tests in English, Mathematics and Science.

Each maintained primary school is required to use a baseline assessment scheme for children at the point of entry and may also use optional tests between the ages when they are a legal requirement.

Reports and references

Teachers must take part in a school's arrangements for compiling reports and references for pupils. Parents of all pupils must receive a report on their child's progress at least once a year. It must cover:

- progress in National Curriculum subjects and other subjects taken
- any public examination results
- National Curriculum assessments results.

The report must show how the pupil's results in GCSE and A level and AS levels compare with the results of the other pupils of the same age in the school and throughout the country. For pupils of compulsory school age, the report must also include an attendance record and details of who the contents of the report can be discussed with.

Participating in meetings arranged for any of the above purposes

Although parents have the right to a significant amount of information about their children's progress, there is no specific legal obligation for teachers to meet parents. It is inconceivable these days that teachers would not meet parents either on organised parents' evenings or through individual arrangements. It is all part of the exercise of the duty of care.

Parents also have a right to attend an annual meeting called by the governors to discuss the statutory governors' annual report.

Teachers have a duty to contribute to the information in the report if requested, but they do not have either the right or duty to attend the annual meeting unless they are parents of a child at the school.

Teachers have a professional obligation to take part in meetings with external bodies although this is not an explicitly legal one. Such meetings, unless undertaken voluntarily, should be part of the time directed by the Head. Teachers then have to attend, and have a duty to participate in, the meeting.

Data Protection

Information about a pupil can be kept in paper form or on a computer, but pupils, like teachers, have a right to know what information about them is being stored. Parents have a right (for a fee) to obtain a copy of most of the personal data held.

Schools are allowed, however, to keep confidential files of social services or medical reports, information which concerns another pupil as well as the one whose information is on file, information about actual or suspected child abuse, and references which are given for the purposes of education, training or employment.

The **Data Protection Act 1998** obliges all those handling personal data to be registered under the Act with the Information Commissioner. The personal information stored must be adequate, relevant and accurate and be obtained for one or more specified uses. Schools must also ensure that they have adequate security arrangements.

The **Data Protection (Subject Access Modification) (Education) Order 2000** provides that in certain cases individuals do not have a right of access to some records.

The school computers used for storing personal information have to be "registered". Independent schools make their own arrangements, but LEAs normally register their schools.

Communicating with Parents and Pupils

Consulting with parents is part of the teacher's professional duty. It has to be done with sensitivity and equity. All schools are now expected to have a formal home/school partnership agreement in place.

Teachers can sometimes lay themselves open to charges of discrimination if too much time is spent on some pupils and not enough on others. Occasionally this leads to complaints being made through the school's complaints procedures.

Parents need to trust teachers and teachers have to earn that trust. This requires understanding and appreciation of parent's concerns.

Independent schools
In independent schools, parents are paying clients and can take their business elsewhere. They can also be sued for outstanding fees. There is, therefore, a contractual bond between the parents and the school. Teachers in independent schools will be expected by their employees to take this relationship seriously.

Maintained schools
In the maintained system, too, parents can choose other schools and since each child is worth public money to the school, it is in everyone's interests for a strong relationship between the school and parents to be fostered.

Defamation

There are times when teachers find it difficult to prevent themselves from telling parents in no uncertain terms what they think of them and/or their child. It is, of course, possible for parents to complain about this and for the teacher to receive disciplinary action.

Sometimes a teacher may be accused of libel and/or slander. Legal suits are often threatened but rarely instigated. Such disputes are usually settled well before a court case gets under way — partly because of time expense and partly because better counsel prevails. However, teachers should know there are limits to what can be written or said — both by teachers and by parents.

In a nutshell, defamation requires a statement to be made which:

- tends to lower the person in the estimation of right-thinking members of society generally
- must be communicated to a third party
- must be false.

Libel is defamation in a permanent form, eg written or recorded. Slander is spoken, ie defamation in an impermanent form. Libel is actionable without proof of damages caused, but slander normally requires proof of damages.

Are there any defences?

The following defences are the most likely in school situations.

1. *Fair comment on a matter of public interest.* Most aspects of education can be considered of public interest and, so long as the person expressing an opinion believes the facts on which the opinion is based to be true, he or she will have a defence.
2. *Justification.* If the statement is true or substantially true, that will be a defence.
3. *Unintentional.* In these cases an apology is usually issued.
4. *Qualified privilege.* This is the most likely defence in school meetings. The statements of teachers and parents engaged in professional discourse are considered to be privileged and unactionable. The defence can only be defeated if the plaintiff could show that the statement was made to another person or persons who did not have a common interest in the subject or that the defendant acted "with malice".

Key stage 4

Parents of pupils in the final year of key stage 4 must be given information, in writing, about the subjects in which the pupil has been awarded a GCSE or other qualification, including the grades given.

Students aged 16 or over

Information on students entered for GCE A level or AS examinations must include the subjects entered by the student and the grades achieved together with the student's overall points score. To calculate a student's point score, the examinations' grades are ascribed the following values:

GCE A Level	GCSE AS Examinations
Grade A — 10 points	Grade A — 5 points
Grade B — 8 points	Grade B — 4 points
Grade C — 6 points	Grade C — 3 points
Grade D — 4 points	Grade D — 2 points
Grade E — 2 points	Grade E — 1 points

Where a student failed to achieve a pass grade or to sit the examination, no points shall be awarded.

Where a pupil has taken both A level and AS examinations, only the A level results shall be taken into account.

A report must also include any International Baccalaureate (IB) diploma or vocational qualification gained by the student.

Underperformance of Pupils

Since 1995, there have been a number of cases coming before the courts alleging negligence in respect of a pupil's performance in school. The courts have concluded that schools not only have a responsibility for pupils' physical well-being, but also for their educational achievement. A Head, and probably a teacher too, owes a duty to take such steps as a reasonable teachers would consider appropriate to deal with evidence of underperformance.

Looking After Pupils' Property

Teachers are often asked to look after pupils' property or might confiscate property from a pupil.

Since taking someone else's property with the intention of permanently depriving them of it constitutes theft, a pupils' property must eventually be given back.

It might be expedient, and perfectly reasonable in many cases, to return the property via the parents.

A teacher will be expected to take reasonable care of a pupil's property and, if they do so, they would not be liable for any loss. However, negligent care of the property resulting in damage or loss might render the teacher liable.

What should I do of I am handed a dangerous or illegal object by a pupil?

If the property turns out to be inherently dangerous or illegal, eg drugs or knives, the police or the parents may be brought in. This would be a matter for senior management. The teacher's duty is to inform the Head. The **Offensive Weapons Act 1996** makes it an offence to carry an offensive weapon or knife on school premises. An offensive weapon is any article made or adapted for causing injury.

Suppose I lose my own property, or it is stolen, can I make a claim for reimbursement of the cost?

Teachers should as a general rule insure their personal property. A school (or LEA) would only responsible if some negligence on their part could be proved. Schools and LEAs often make *ex gratia* payments to teachers for loss of or damage to personal property.

Collection of Money

Teachers often have to collect money from children for a variety of reasons. Such monies should be sent to the bursar or school secretary as soon as possible. They should never be put into a teacher's own bank account.

Money received should always be acknowledged with a written receipt.

Control of Pupil Behaviour

Circular 10/99 *Social Exclusion: Pupil Support* contains the Secretary of State's guidance on pupil attendance, behaviour, exclusion and reintegration. The focus of the guidance is on raising educational achievement for those pupils who are disaffected, or failing to participate fully in the school experience through difficult behaviour or poor attendance. Schools will be expected to have strategies in place to identify and meet the needs of pupils who require help in order to avoid truancy and disaffection.

Schools will also have to ensure they have the training and the alternative strategies to cope with disruptive behaviour. Schools will still be able to exclude disruptive pupils, but exclusion must be a last resort and permanent exclusion must only be contemplated for very serious disruption.

School behaviour policies

Schools will have to have policies in place identifying the actions and alternatives available to staff. For difficult groups of pupils, there should be an educational programme which is constantly reviewed. The eventual aim is to restore the disaffected pupil to the classroom.

Pastoral support programme

Circular 10/99 introduced the idea of a pastoral support programme (PSP) for pupils whose behaviour becomes too difficult for the other measures. As well as setting clear targets for pupils, the PSP will also act as a detailed record for governors. Where a pupil has been permanently excluded, the PSP must be submitted to the governing body as part of the school's evidence of its attempts to alter the pupil's behaviour.

Discipline

Teachers are obliged to maintain good order and discipline, safeguard pupils' health and safety both on the premises and when engaged on school activities elsewhere.

The duty to ensure good discipline in the school is the Head's, aided by staff. Section 61 of the **School Standards and Framework Act 1998** sets out the duties of heads of maintained schools in relation to pupil discipline.

Governing bodies of maintained schools have to ensure that policies designed to promote good behaviour and discipline of pupils are in place. They must also have written statements on the general principles to which a Head should have regard in determining disciplinary measures in the school, having consulted the Head and parents of registered pupils.

The Head has to promote self-discipline and proper regard for authority, encourage good behaviour and respect for others, secure acceptable standards of behaviour and regulate conduct, having regard to the governing body's written statement.

How does a teacher know what the standard of behaviour should be?

It is up to the Head to set out the standards which are expected. These will usually have been agreed in consultation with staff. At least once a year, the Head must bring the school's disciplinary measures to the attention of persons employed in the school (in addition to pupils and parents).

Schools should, therefore, have behaviour policies which are clear, specific, reasonable, constructive and with a minimum of rules. Punishments for bad behaviour should be included (Circular 10/99).

Teachers must act in accordance with the policies.

Can I refuse to teach a disruptive pupil?

Schools should all have clear policies on how to handle pupils whose behaviour is threatening. It would be inadvisable for an individual teacher to take unilateral action.

Where there is a clash of opinion between teachers and the school authorities, teachers should take collective action through their unions.

In a recent case, *P v National Union of Schoolmasters/Union of Women Teachers* 2001, the Court upheld a union's right to ballot members on refusing to teach P in the normal classroom setting. The judge confirmed that a school is entitled to put a disruptive pupil in a separate classroom, so long as it is for sound educational reasons. However, it would be unreasonable if the school was to segregate a pupil simply to comply with a whimsical request made by teachers.

Punishment

Sometimes the concepts of *discipline* and *punishment* become blurred. They can at times be used synonymously. Discipline in educational circles is the desired outcome of teachers' effect on pupils. Punishment is one of the means of achieving this state.

The responsibility for the day-to-day discipline in the school rests with the Head. Heads must promote self-discipline and proper regard for authority, encourage good behaviour among pupils and regulate conduct.

Teachers too have a duty, under the new conditions of employment, to maintain good order and discipline.

How do I know what punishment to use?

The punishment or sanctions allowed by a school should be set out in the school's prospectus and should be communicated to staff, usually via the staff handbook. Teachers must stick to these sanctions and not introduce their own.

The general principles were succinctly expounded by Mr Justice Phillimore in *Mansell v Griffiths* (1908) who stated that it is enough for a teacher to say that the punishment which he or she administered was moderate; that it was not driven by any bad motive but was such as is usual within the school; and it was the kind of punishment that a parent of a child might expect the child to receive if the child behave badly.

Detention Teachers have a right to deprive children of their liberty by virtue of their position *in loco parentis* (otherwise it would constitute kidnapping, a criminal offence) so long as detention is a normal punishment in the school.

The **Education Act 1997** allows schools to detain pupils outside school hours without parental consent. However, a number of conditions must be satisfied, the main one being that the parents must have been informed in writing at least 24 hours previously. There is information about the law on detention and how to apply it in Circular 10/99.

Can I keep a whole class in detention?

At one time, whole class detentions were a common way of sharing out punishment for unruly behaviour when culprits were difficult to pinpoint. Since the case of *Terrington v Lancashire C.C.* (1986) this is now more problematic. Mr Terrington claimed damages for the false imprisonment of his son who had been kept in detention with the rest of his class some 10 minutes after school. The registrar decided that it did amount to false imprisonment but that in the circumstances it was justified. He accepted that sometimes blanket detention might be necessary.

On appeal to the county court, the judge also decided that, although punishment should not be indiscriminate and blanket detention should only be used as a last resort, it would be reasonable in certain circumstances to hold a whole class responsible for indiscipline.

As a rule of thumb, whole classes should only be detained during school time, for example at break, or with the permission of the Head after school. It would be the Head's responsibility to make the necessary arrangements with parents, even though in practice the actual organisation might be delegated.

Exclusions In maintained schools, only the Head has a power to exclude a pupil from school for disciplinary reasons. This is usual in independent schools too.

There are two types of exclusion: fixed period and permanent.

1. Fixed period: fixed period exclusions can be for periods not exceeding 15 days in aggregate in any term. The limit on the number of days a pupil can be excluded from school in any one year is 45 days.
2. Permanent exclusions: the Head excludes, but normally only after a range of alternative strategies has been tried. A pupil is unlikely to be permanently excluded for a first or one-off offence, unless there was a very serious context. The Secretary of State has advised appeal panels that it would not be appropriate to direct re-instatement if the circumstances included violence, a severe threat of violence, sexual abuse or the pupil presented a significant risk to others in the school by selling illegal drugs.

Parents (and pupils if over 18) can appeal to the governing body's Discipline Committee which can direct the Head to re-instate the pupil, or uphold the exclusion. Parents can then appeal to an independent panel set up by the LEA. This panel has to have a regard to the Secretary of State's guidance concerning the circumstances in which it would not be appropriate to direct re-instatement.

The **School Standard and Framework Act 1998** requires Heads, governors, LEAs and appeal panels to have regard to the guidance on exclusions in Circular 10/99 in discharging their functions in relation to pupil exclusions.

An implication of recent European Human Rights' legislation, which includes the "right to education", is that schools will have to set and mark work for an excluded pupil.

Can a teacher refuse to teach a pupil who has been reinstated against the Head's and teachers' advice?

Much concern has been shown in recent years by teachers who feel that certain pupils have been unjustifiably returned to the school where they have been unacceptably violent. It is an emotive issue and each case shows up a host of conflicting perspectives and emotions.

The law is clear — it states that teachers who refuse to teach a pupil properly registered at, and admitted to, the school are in breach of contract.

Against this it can be argued that such pupils are a potential risk to the health and safety of staff. Employees are protected by employment legislation when taking reasonable action on the grounds of health and safety.

In the end, it is not the law which resolves such conflicts but negotiation and agreed plans of action. These rarely satisfy all parties but resolutions have to be found in the end for the sake of the remainder of the pupils.

Corporal punishment Following European Court of Justice judgments on this matter, British law was changed. By a narrow majority, a "free vote" in 1986 resulted in the banning of corporal punishment in maintained schools during the passage of the Education Bill, which became the **Education (No. 2) Act 1986**. Section 47 of the Act covers the abolition of corporal punishment. This is now contained in s.131 of the **School Standards and Framework Act 1998**.

Both formal caning and casual hitting of children by teachers and other employees in the school are illegal even though parents may do it. Slapping, prodding, shaking, chalk-flicking, board-duster throwing and ruler flicking, are all examples of banned forms of chastisement.

The **Education Act 1997** has inserted a new section, s.550A into the 1996 Act. This states that a teacher or other member of the school staff may use reasonable force in order to prevent a pupil from:

- committing an offence
- causing personal injury or damage (including to themselves)
- engaging in any activity prejudicial to the maintenance of good order, whether during a lesson or at any other time.

For example, if a teacher walked into a room and saw two pupils about to throw another out of a window, he or she would be within his or her rights to grab hold of them. It would be the teacher's duty to try to prevent any injury.

DfES Circular 10/98 *Section 550A of the Education Act 1996: The use of force to control or restrain pupils* gives other examples of when physical intervention might be appropriate and factors that teachers should bear in mind before deciding to intervene.

Teachers should not hesitate to act in such an emergency but it is true that there is a fine line between punishment and preventing danger.

In addition, any physical intervention has to be with reasonable force. If the physical restrain is excessive, whether or not it constitutes punishment, then a teacher lays himself or herself open to criminal as well as civil proceedings.

In practice, it is not common for criminal charges to be laid, although it does happen occasionally. Where a teacher oversteps the mark it is usually a matter for internal disciplinary proceedings.

The abolition of corporal punishment applies to independent as well as maintained schools.

Pupil intervention units The Government has provided funds to schools to set up their own facilities to meet the needs of pupils whose behaviour is likely to damage their own progress and that of others, and who run the risk of permanent exclusion from the school. The recommendation is that schools should set up on-site facilities to provide specialist support to these students.

How will a court judge the reasonableness of a teacher's action?

The test that a court is likely to apply is that of "reasonably foreseeable". A court will judge whether, in all the circumstances, a teacher could have reasonably foreseen the possible consequences of a particular action or lack of action.

The following cases concerning negligence will reveal the fine discrimination between one set of facts and another.

A seven-year-old blind boy was injured while playing in a hostel for blind children when a child with full sight jumped on his back without warning. The judge held that the incident could not have been foreseen, even if the matron had been in the room at the time. It was "a thing of the moment" and no-one was found to be negligent — *Gow v Glasgow Education Authority.* (1992).

On the other hand, when some pupils broke into a conservatory in their residential school and were injured by phosphorous which they found in a bottle, the court help the school liable. The judge remarked that it was evidently negligent to leave a bottle of phosphorous lying about in a place accessible to pupils "knowing what boys are like" — *Williams v Eady* (1893).

During a school break, some boys found some elastic bands in a waste paper basket which they proceeded to use as a catapult. The elastic struck another pupil in the eye — blinding that eye. The teachers on duty were at another part of their patrol at the time. The judge considered the leaving of elastic in an open basket amounted to a failure in the standard of care required. It was possible to foresee that an injury could be caused and if the system of supervision had worked properly, the accident might not have happened — *Beaumont v Surrey* C.C. (1968).

Will I be negligent if I leave my class unattended for a few minutes?

Normally, teachers try not to leave classes totally unsupervised. If a teacher had to leave in order to, for example, speak to a pupil or teacher outside the room, or to fetch something she or he had forgotten, consideration should be given to the age, aptitude and general nature of the group, the expected time away, and the proximity of other teachers before deciding whether they can be left on their own for a few minutes.

In *Ahmed v City of Glasgow Council* (2000), a secondary pupil suffered an eye injury by an eraser thrown by another pupil when the teacher had left the class for ten minutes. Both the first Court and the Appeal Court dismissed the pupil's claim for damages. The Court's view was that a teacher must exercise care and forethought, having regard to the children's age, inexperience, carelessness and high spirits. Fault however, could only be established if the incident was more likely to happen after a period of absence. The Appeal judge considered that such an incident as this one is not unusual in classroom life and could have occurred if the teacher was there and his or her back was turned.

Can teachers be sued for negligence?

It is unlikely that a teacher would be sued individually for negligence for the simple reason that the teacher is not likely to have the financial resources of the employer. In any case, the employee is insured against any damages arising from negligence in the course of employment.

The employer, LEA or governing body, or employees acting as their servant may be sued, but only one sum can be awarded as damages. If a teacher is a joint defendant, the sum can be apportioned. The only occasion when a teacher might have to be responsible for his or her own negligence is when he or she has acted outside the terms of the contract and recklessly done something that should not have been done.

First Aid

According to health and safety legislation, every workplace where there are at least 50 employees must have a trained first aider. There is no mention of non-employees such as pupils. Consequently, schools with fewer than 50 employees are not required by law to have a first aider on the premises. Most schools assume, however, that their duty of care requires them to make first aid provision.

PE and sports teachers will find it highly desirable to have a first aid qualification which is regularly updated.

All teachers, especially those in charge of pupils in dangerous places such as sports halls, laboratories and workshops should know the emergency procedures in the event of an accident and know where the nearest first aid help can be obtained.

Should an accident occur, a teacher in charge should know how to take charge of the situation, keep everyone calm, assess the injury and the circumstances and determine a course of action, taking into account the needs of the other pupils in the group.

In January 1998, the DfES published a very helpful document, *Guidance on First Aid for Schools*. In the unlikely event of a major disaster, each LEA has a contingency plan which every school should be aware of.

Medicines in Schools

Teachers should never administer medicines to a pupil off their own bat, nor give permission to pupils to take medicines.

Schools should have policies (often following LEA guidelines) covering the administration of medicines. These should be strictly followed.

Teachers are not obliged by law nor by their contract to administer medicines to pupils or supervise pupils taking medicines. It is a voluntary action. Support staff may, however, have such duties to provide medical assistance as part of their contracts. Employers should ensure that their insurance policies contain appropriate cover for staff willing to administer medication.

However, teachers have a common law duty to act *in loco parentis* as a reasonably prudent parent would to ensure that pupils are healthy and safe on school premises. As a general rule, school staff should not administer medication without first receiving appropriate information and/or training. In exceptional circumstances, however, administering medicine might be a necessary emergency action. This would also be the case if the teacher was in charge of an activity off-site.

Normally, it is the child's parents who are responsible for their child's medication. A Head may decide that the school can assist in this. Usually such a decision will be made in order to encourage regular attendance at the school and participation in school life. Heads would seek advice and guidance before making such a decision and would ensure that only staff who were qualified to assist, and had agreed to do so, would be called upon.

General guidance and specific guidance on the medication and control of asthma, epilepsy, diabetes and anaphylaxis are contained in Circular 14/96 *Supporting Pupils with Medical Needs* and the accompanying guidance *Supporting Pupils with Medical Needs: A Good Practice Guide*.

Personal Errands

A teacher should take care before sending a pupil on a personal errand, eg to go shopping or make a cup of tea.

According to a case decided in 1911, teachers should not be prevented from asking children to do "small acts of courtesy", but the teacher would have to ensure the child was not put into any jeopardy (personal or legal).

It is likely to be wrong to ask a small child to make a cup of tea unsupervised, but not an older child. It would certainly be wrong to ask a child under 16 to buy cigarettes since that would be illegal.

Children in Trouble

Children who are showing signs of distress cause anxiety to teachers, who are obviously closely placed and able to observe signs of neglect, abuse, bereavement, etc.

Teachers should know who the *designated person* is on the staff whose role it is to liaise with social services on these matters. Schools should also have a policy on how such cases are to be dealt with.

Bullying

In *Bradford-Smart v West Sussex County Council* (2000), bullying was defined as "conduct intended to cause hurt, either physical or psychological, which is unprovoked and which continues over a long period."

Bullying has always been present in schools but it should not be tolerated. Some bullies are themselves victims of forms of abuse or neglect. Bullying may be racist in nature.

The 1989 Elton Report on *Discipline in Schools* recommended that schools should:

- be alert to signs of bullying
- deal firmly with all such behaviour

- have clear rules with appropriate sanctions
- make it clear that pupils also have a responsibility to share with staff any knowledge about cases of bullying.

A number of cases which have come to the courts in 2000 and 2001 emphasised the requirement for teachers to "exercise the skills of an ordinary teacher" in tackling bullying. In particular, schools are expected to:

- have clear policies known by all
- investigate instances promptly
- keep colleagues informed of incidents
- monitor the agreed strategies
- keep adequate records.

Pupils with emotional and behavioural difficulties

Teachers often have nightmares about children in their charge who have severe emotional and behavioural difficulties. It probably causes more stress than any other aspect of a teacher's job.

It is understandable for teachers to feel isolated when nothing they do or recommend to alleviate the problems caused by such pupils seems appreciated.

Heads have a responsibility to see that colleagues are helped in every possible way to find strategies that take account of the pupils difficulties while bearing in mind the needs of the rest of the class — and the teacher.

Teachers themselves should take advice, devise their own strategies and, finally, if necessary, admit defeat. It is at this point that Heads must exercise their duty to ensure good behaviour and tackle the problem.

Increasingly, Heads have felt it necessary to support staff by excluding a pupil permanently. It is then up to the governors and LEA whether they will support the Head and staff or direct reinstatement and risk confrontation.

The LEA may, if it wishes, send a pupil to a Pupil Referral Unit (PRU) where alternative education to that provided by the school should be on offer. The LEA could also offer home tuition on a full-time or part-time basis.

Both these strategies are expensive, however, and in many LEAs the statutory PRU provision is too little.

Circular 9/94 *The Education of Children with Emotional and Behavioural Difficulties* aims to give practical guidance to schools.

Child Protection and Child Abuse

The **Children Act 1989** places a duty on local authorities to safeguard the welfare of children in their area. Teachers by virtue of the duty of care must also safeguard children's health and safety.

All schools will have systems for detecting and reporting any signs of absence or neglect of children. All teachers have a duty to report any signs of abuse to a senior member of staff, as laid down in the school procedures.

A system of regional co-ordinators for child protection has been introduced. These posts will link with Area Child Protection Committees (ACPCs) and other local networks. They will improve the support and guidance available to schools, and will be able to spread good practice.

Any member of staff who suspects that a pupil might be suffering abuse from a member of staff should report it in strict confidence to the Head. This may even be a relatively minor incident, such as a teacher shaking a pupil, as it could cause injury or be an indicator for more serious abuse. While this is a difficult and sensitive area, it is better that incidents are reported and investigated sensitively rather than suspicions be allowed to fester. Mistakes or inaccurate interpretations are less likely to occur if matters are dealt with promptly.

In responding to a pupil who makes an allegation a teacher must not promise confidentiality, but must take into account the child's age and understanding, and whether the child may be at risk.

Reporting Allegations

All schools should have a senior member of staff with specific responsibility for co-ordinating action within the school, and for liaising with social services and other agencies. The Government Document *Working Together to Safeguard Children 1999* sets out the responsibilities.

Schools must also have a "Nominated Governor" (the chair, or in the absence of the chair, the vice chair) responsible for liaising with the Head and designated teacher.

Teachers should report allegations to the Head, or to the designated teacher if the allegations are made against the Head.

The Head and designated LEA officer will consult urgently about any allegation about the action to be taken.

Where the allegation refers to the use of reasonable force or is found to be false, it would be appropriate for the Head to deal with the matter.

If the allegation is of assault beyond the use of reasonable force then the local child protection procedures will be used.

Restriction of Employment
The **Restriction of Employment (Amendment) Regulations 2001** allow the Secretary of State to refer certain cases concerning allegations against teachers to the General Teaching Council.

Such cases will be ones where it has been alleged that a teacher has been guilty of unacceptable professional conduct or where the teacher has been convicted of a relevant offence, and the circumstances do not give rise to any issues concerning the safety and welfare of persons under the age of 19.

What about malicious false allegations?

Children do make false allegations. Teachers are particularly vulnerable to allegations of abuse. Allegations can be mischievous, misplaced or malicious. *Working Together Under the Children Act* suggests three possible strands to an investigation of alleged abuse:

1. The child protection investigation.
2. The police investigation.
3. A disciplinary investigation.

What happens after the initial assessment?

There are four possible outcomes.

1. If the pupil making the allegation is likely to suffer harm an immediate referral under the local child protection procedures is made.
2. If the allegation is of a criminal offence a referral would be made.
3. The allegation may represent inappropriate behaviour or poor practice by the teacher (outside the above categories), which need to be considered under the school's disciplinary procedures.
4. The allegation is false.

What happens if there is no apparent foundation for the allegations?

The Head in consultation with the designated teacher and LEA officer will consider if the child is suffering problems at all. The Head will inform the teacher in writing of the allegations and that no action is to be taken. Counselling, or informal advice, may be offered to the teacher. The child's parents will be informed, and may receive counselling and support. A report will be prepared by the Head giving reasons for the conclusion.

What happens if there appears to be some substance to the allegations?

The Head or governing body may consider suspending the teacher, but suspension is not automatic. If the case is referred to the local child protection agencies, and disciplinary action is not contemplated, suspension is more likely. Before making the decision the Head or nominated governor will consult the LEA officer and consider any recommendation made by the child protection agency.

Suspension would only be undertaken with "good reason", which might include:

- where a child is at risk
- where the allegations are so serious that dismissal for gross misconduct is possible
- where it is necessary to facilitate the investigation.

When suspension is being considered the teacher will be interviewed and could be accompanied by a trade union official or a "friend". An opportunity to make representations will be given.

The teacher is entitled to as much information as is consistent with not interfering with the investigation. If as a result the Head or chair of governors considers that suspension is necessary the teacher will be informed immediately, and written confirmation despatched within one working day.

During the suspension the teacher should have the name of an LEA officer as an information contact. The investigations must be conducted with due speed, and meanwhile the teacher or his or her representative should be contacted regularly with information.

If the teacher is not suspended, support should be offered.

At the end of an investigation a meeting should be arranged, and the teacher should be informed of the next steps.

What happens at the end of the investigation if misconduct is proved?

The teacher would be subject to the school's disciplinary procedures and might be dismissed, or resign. He or she might also be faced with a criminal charge.

Records of the investigation and of the outcome should be retained.

The Head will report the case to the DfES's misconduct section.

Some LEAs (schools) issue codes of conduct for employees whose work brings them into contact with young people. The aim is to minimise the risk of improper behaviour.

Employees should:

- be aware of the dangers arising from private interviews with pupils
- avoid meetings with pupils away from school premises, unless specifically approved by the Head or senior staff
- ensure that some other adult knows a private meeting is taking place
- be aware of the dangers of administering first aid involving physical contact; someone else should be present whenever possible
- report as quickly as possible any situation that might be misconstrued — particularly when a teacher has had to restrain a pupil physically, and where a complain has been made by a pupil or parent
- use their discretion about comforting or reassuring a child in distress; in itself this is acceptable as it is such as a caring parent would do, but there are dangers of misconstruction and it is better if someone else was nearby
- try not to make gratuitous physical contact with a pupil, eg putting a hand on the shoulder or arm
- remember that any form of physical punishment is unlawful and that a physical response to misbehaviour is also unlawful, unless it is intended to restrain the pupil to prevent some harm occurring
- use discretion in conversations that cover sensitive matters

- judge whether it is appropriate to give counselling or advice if approached by a particular pupil in distress, referring them to someone with direct pastoral responsibility for the child might be one response
- avoid encouraging discussion amongst pupils which could be construed as having a sexual connotation, unless this is clearly necessary in the context of the lesson, eg a health education lesson or biology lesson, or discussions on a piece of literature in the school's syllabus.

School Duties Before and After School

Teachers are required to supervise children for a reasonable time before, during and after school sessions.

Children tend to arrive at school any time up to half an hour before school begins (in a few cases even earlier). Many also stay on site for activities up to an hour after school and even those who leave immediately can take 10 minutes or more to leave the site.

The courts have made it clear that just because pupils arrive on the school site does not mean that schools must provide supervision.

Therefore, schools make clear in prospectuses the official opening and closing times and between these times the Head has to provide proper supervision.

Schools differ in how they tackle this but normally there is a duty roster with timings, specified areas to be patrolled, responsibilities of teachers on duty and emergency drills.

Teachers must take these duties as seriously as teaching duties. They should not be delegated to anyone else without permission from the senior staff in charge of the duties.

How long can I be required to be on duty before and after school?

There can be no definitive statement as to how long supervision must be provided before or after school.

Heads are enabled by their conditions of employment to direct teachers' supervision duties as long as it is reasonable. Heads have a responsibility to ensure that the number of teachers on duty is adequate for the purposes.

Whatever time is allocated must be included in the teacher's "time budget" under the regulations concerning "working time" (see above).

Departure of pupils from school

It is usual for teachers to supervise, via a duty roster, the departure of pupils from the school. The Head lays down the arrangements and determines the amount of time it should take. The rule-of-thumb figure is 10 minutes.

However, if the children are young and are usually picked up by parents, teachers have a duty to assist the Head in keeping them securely on site until the parents pick them up.

Sometimes schools have a procedure for handing children over to parents and, if so, teachers must adhere to this.

Any such changes in timings should be allowed for in teachers' "directed time" budgets.

Where does a teacher's responsibility stop?

It is tempting to be precise and say, "at the school gate", but this is not strictly true, although it is a useful guideline.

However, if a teacher sees a group of pupils outside the school gates acting in a way likely to cause a risk to themselves or others, the teacher has a duty to exercise control.

This amounts to exercising a quick risk assessment and professional judgment about the best way to react.

Can a teacher stop traffic to allow pupils to cross roads?

A teacher has no particular authority nor duty to stop traffic in order to allow children to cross roads. Where the requirement is to cross a road outside the school, then the LEA or governing body should provide crossing wardens where there is any likely risk.

If the situation arises where teachers are escorting pupils outside school, the journey should be planned to take in authorised crossing places (zebra or pelican crossings). If this is not possible, teachers should advise the Head, whose job it is to determine the most expedient and safe method.

A teacher could be blamed if an accident happens as a result of trying to control traffic.

Common sense usually dictates what is the right course of action in the circumstances.

Teachers should avoid taking large groups along a road without pavements. Sometimes, as in the case of parades or large groups going to church services, it cannot be avoided. There are strict police regulations about how this should be managed. Heads will brief staff, who should then follow the arrangements.

In all these situations, teachers have to ensure orderly behaviour. If a "crocodile" of children forces a passer-by off a pavement, the supervisory teachers would have some of the liability for any injury.

Can schools release children from school early?

Heads can release children early but must inform parents and LEAs if intending to do so. The case of *Barnes v Hampshire C.C.* (1969) held that the release of a very young child before the official end of the school day was taking an unnecessary risk. In this case, an accident occurred and the LEA was sued for negligence.

Does a teacher have a duty to supervise a young child, say an infant, while waiting for an older sibling to arrive?

There is no contractual requirement to do so. The Head of the infant school has to rely on voluntary help from staff or make arrangements with the senior school to supervise them, or failing that, to advise parents that they must make the arrangements.

If the parents fail to do so, the matter should go to the education welfare officer.

Bus duties
If a school bus comes onto the site, the school must see that pupils board and alight from the bus in an orderly and safe manner. Teachers must take part in any school procedures for this.

Minibuses

Many schools operate minibuses and, so long as they carry passengers who do not pay a fare, then the school is free from the duties of the public passenger network licensing. By virtue of the provision of the **Minibus Act 1977**, as consolidated in s.19 of the **Transport Act 1985**, schools can recoup operating costs but not make a profit.

The school must have a permit for the bus and must ensure roadworthiness and the fitness of drivers. Insurance companies usually ensure that staff are experienced drivers before insuring them to drive a school minibus.

Driver requirements
Drivers must normally be medically fit and must pass an appropriate test if they wish to drive a minibus. However, volunteer drivers are exempt, provided that they are 21 year or older and have held a licence for at least two years.

Minibus Safety: A Code of Practice has been published to help schools and other organisations to ensure a consistent safety-based approach to the running of a minibus.

Drivers must follow the EC Driver Hours Rules when on trips abroad. For journeys in the UK there are no rules for minibuses driven by volunteers, but there are for paid drivers. The Code of Practice recommends driving hours, which schools are urged to follow.

What is the teacher-driver responsible for?

Drivers are responsible for:

- ensuring that they hold a valid licence
- checking roadworthiness before setting out
- knowing the safety discipline required
- ensuring the safety of the passengers
- ensuring that each child is fastened in with a seat-belt (or disabled person's harness)
- stopping driving when not fully capable through tiredness or other reason, keeping to the school's rules about driving periods.

School Inspections

LEA inspections

LEAs, in fulfilling their duty towards their schools and the community, are entitled to receive information and can inspect a school in order to obtain this information.

They may also provide an inspection service for schools in or out of their area for a fee payable by the school.

OFSTED inspections

Schools are inspected by the Office for Standards in Education (OFSTED) under the **Schools Inspections Act 1996** and the **Education Act 1997** and the **School Standards and Framework Act 1998**. The revised OFSTED Framework, *Inspecting Schools*, governs all inspections, and inspectors are expected to stick to its provisions (further details are contained on page 10).

Every school will be inspected at least once in a six-year cycle, but some schools will only have a "short inspection", which is aimed at the most effective schools.

Inspection teams are led by a Registered Inspector (RgI), who will be appointed following tenders for each inspection. The RgI will choose his or her team from a list of trained inspectors.

Schools will have between six and ten weeks notice of an inspection. Prior to the inspection week a considerable amount of documentation will have to be provided by the school, and the RgI will make a preliminary visit.

Before and/or during the inspection the RgI and possibly other inspectors will meet both governors and parents as well as staff.

Teachers are obliged to allow inspectors into their classes and to provide any information that inspectors might reasonably request.

Teachers have no right to a debrief after an inspection of a lesson but inspectors often find time to do this, if they can.

Oral debriefings are offered to department heads and senior management teams and the governing body. Eventually a written report is sent to the school. This report is accompanied by a summary and both have to be made available to the public. Schools must also send a copy of the summary of the report to all parents within 10 days of its receipt.

The report will contain numerous recommendations.

What happens after the receipt of an OFSTED report?

The relevant body has to prepare an action plan within 40 working days. The plan should take into account the findings of the inspectors, their recommendations and the school's own development plan.

This action plan is sent to OFSTED and the relevant body.

The governing body of a maintained school, except for nursery schools, must include a statement in its annual governors' report indicating the state of implementation of the action plan.

Schools requiring special measures

If a RgI believes that a school is not providing an acceptable standard of education, he or she must say so to the governing body and report to Her Majesty's Chief Inspector (HMCI).

If HMCI agrees, then special measures for that school will be prescribed.

An action plan will be drawn up and its progress will be monitored by Her Majesty's Inspectors (HMI), usually once per term.

When the school shows significant improvement, it will no longer be considered to require these special measures.

CONTINUING PROFESSIONAL DEVELOPMENT

Although teachers do not have a contractual 'right' to continuing professional development (CPD), their annual performance review (appraisal) is expected to generate some priorities for further learning. In fact, the best schools stimulate and support the learning of adults as well as children and young people. Many, now have accreditation as Investors in People (IIP).

Schools have access to a range of resources for CPD, including Standards Funding (which comes to them from central government) and the New Opportunities Fund (NOF) for ICT training for serving teachers. Teachers should expect to get their fair share of these resources.

New Strategy

During 2001, the DfES launched a new strategy for CPD, *Learning and Teaching* (DfES Reference: 0071/2001). Further information about the materials and opportunities available can be found on the DfES website: *www.dfes.gov.uk/teachers/professional_development*

Teaching Information and Communications Technology

All NQTs now have to be computer literate to mandatory standards in order to receive Qualified Teacher Status. By 2002 serving teachers are expected to be competent to teach using information and communications technology (ICT) in the curriculum. Competency in and understanding of the use of ICT should be seen as a high value in the delivery of each subject cirriculum, and as leading to career enhancement.

The training of teachers in ICT has been funded by the New Opportunities Fund. The main thrust has been to enable teachers to appreciate the value of making use of ICT to enhance teaching and learning.

A REASONABLE WORKING ENVIRONMENT

Teachers should expect to work in a reasonable environment, both for teaching and to undertake their own preparation and marking. There should now be some earmarked funds available to improve school buildings and staff facilities.

CHAPTER 5

THE CURRICULUM

THE GENERAL CURRICULUM

Each maintained school in England and Wales must have a balanced, broadly-based curriculum which promotes the spiritual, moral, cultural, mental and physical development of pupils and prepares pupils for the opportunities, responsibilities and experiences of adult life.

The school's curriculum consists of a number of elements:

- the National Curriculum, from years 1 to 11
- Religious Education, which must be offered from years 1 to 13
- other courses not in the National Curriculum which the school can include at its discretion, for example Economics, Sociology, Latin.

The full curriculum of a school could also, paradoxically, be said to include so-called "extra-curricular" activities.

Each department determines how the National Curriculum and other subjects are to be taught. Precisely how the decision is reached depends on the ethos of the school. In most cases, subject/classroom teachers will be involved in the discussions. Sometimes it is inevitable that teachers have to take on existing arrangements.

THE NATIONAL CURRICULUM

The National Curriculum runs from the pre-Reception class to Year 11 (16 year olds) The "foundation stage" is for pupils aged three until the Reception year and has early learning goals. The National Curriculum is made up of nine foundation subjects in primary schools and ten in secondary schools. Three of them are *core subjects* — English, Mathematics and Science (and Welsh in Wales) and Information and

Communication Technology (ICT). The other subjects are Technology, History, Geography, a Modern Foreign Language (in secondary schools), Art and Design, Music and PE. In addition all pupils in the school must study Religious Education.

The core curriculum at key stages 1 and 2 in maintained schools is now — English, Mathematics, Science, ICT and Religious Education.

In 2000 the National Curriculum was extensively revised. A key focus is now to ensure that all pupils develop literacy and numeracy skills and have access to a broad and balanced curriculum, which will provide them with a body of knowledge and the skills to inspire a commitment to life-long learning.

There is a new common structure and design for all subjects. Each subject for each key stage contains the programme of study with two requirements:

- knowledge, skills and understanding
- breadth of study.

Each programme of study contains attainment targets against which each pupil's progress is measured. There are eight level descriptions for each attainment target. Teachers are required to describe their assessment of their pupils' achievements by choosing the "best fit" description.

Pupils are expected to spend more time on literacy and numeracy in key stages 1 and 2.

Pupils in Years 9–11 have a right to careers education. Circular 5/97 *Careers Education and Guidance in Schools: Effective Partnerships with Career Services* gives detailed guidance.

Programmes of study for Citizenship will also be introduced in 2002, which will be non-statutory for pupils in key stages 1 and 2, but is recommended as the minimum entitlement for pupils in primary schools. There is also a non-statutory programme of study for Personal, Social and Health Education (PSHE).

More flexibility has been built into the National Curriculum by the **Education Act 2002** which includes measures to tailor education provision more closely to individual talents and aspirations.

Assessment

Pupils move through four key stages according to age. Key stage 1 is for 5–7 year olds (years 1 and 2), key stage 2 is for 7–11 year olds (years 3–6), key stage 3 is for 11–14 year olds (years 7–9) and key stage 4 is for 14–16 year olds (years 10 and 11). The Sixth Form (years 12 and 13) is often called key stage 5.

Pupils are assessed at four points in key stages 1–4. For most of them, this will be at 7, 11, 14 and 16, but some pupils will be accelerated.

At the end of key stages 1–3, pupils will be assessed through teacher assessment, but in some subjects external National Curriculum tests (commonly called SATs) will also be set. Where both are included, they have equal weighting. Both must be reported to parents.

From key stage 1 to key stage 3, pupils' performance is measured in levels 1 to 8, with an extra level above 8 for pupils who show exceptional performance.

National analyses and "performance tables" of results are published and booklets of school-by-school results are published on a regional basis. These are passed on to parents via the school.

Schools must publish their own sets of results in school prospectuses and governors' annual reports.

At key stage 4, the assessment is carried out normally through the General Certificate of Secondary Education (GCSE). There is no legal requirement concerning which subjects should be taken at GCSE, but no course leading to a qualification may be provided in maintained schools unless they have been approved by the Secretary of State. A list of these appears annually in the Circular *Statutory Approval of Qualifications under s.5 of the Education Reform Act 1988*.

GCSE gradings run from G to A, with A* for exceptional work and U for ungraded.

Teaching ICT

The revised National Curriculum in 2000 includes ICT as one of the six key skills embedded in the National Curriculum. The key skill includes the ability to use a range of information sources and ICT tools to find, analyse, interpret, evaluate and present information for a range of purposes.

Current developments in ICT focus on making use of the National Grid for Learning (NGfL). The aim of the NGfL is to provide a national focus for harnessing new technologies in order to raise educational standards. It is part of the Government's initiative to connect all schools, colleges, universities and libraries to the Internet.

Is every pupil expected to take all National Curriculum subjects?

Heads are allowed to disapply or modify the National Curriculum for individual pupils for up to six months. It can be for a longer period if the pupil has major educational difficulties and a statement of special needs is drawn up which includes a recommendation to modify or disapply the National Curriculum requirements. Under SEN regulations, a pupil's statement of special educational needs could include disapplication of single or multiple subjects or the entire National Curriculum.

Schools can also apply to the Secretary of State to be allowed to disapply or modify the National Curriculum requirements for the whole school or particular groups in order to undertake development work or experiments.

Following the **Education Act 2002** more flexibility will be introduced.

Where can I find the National Curriculum?

The revised National Curriculum is contained in the document The National Curriculum which all schools have.

Each subject department in a school will order its own syllabus accordingly ensuring that the requirements for each key stage are fulfilled at the appropriate time.

The National Curriculum is content-orientated. It does not set out to tell teachers how to teach their subject. The methodology is a matter for the school, the department and individual teachers.

Is the National Curriculum all that has to be taught up to 16?

The National Curriculum is designed notionally to leave up to 25% of time for other subjects — notably Religious Education, which is not part of the National Curriculum but is compulsory for all pupils (up to Year 13 in fact) whose parents have not opted them out.

Other curriculum activities will undoubtedly find their way into each school's curriculum. Personal and social education in one form or another is almost a certainty. Study skills, business studies, economics, international understanding, careers education, health and environment education are all likely to figure somewhere.

In 2002, Personal, Social and Health Education and Citizenship education became part of the curriculum entitlement for each student. Personal, Social and Health Education will be non-statutory. Citizenship will be a statutory requirement in the secondary curriculum, but not in the primary school curriculum.

In Wales

Significant differences exist between the English and Welsh National Curriculum orders. The unique difference is the teaching of Welsh as a core or foundation subject, but there are variations in many other subject areas. These will be reflected in Welsh schools' specific programmes of study.

Key Stage 4

All 14–16 year olds have to study English, Mathematics, Science and Physical Education and at least short courses in Technology, Information Technology and a Modern Foreign Language. History, Geography, Art and Music are not compulsory. Information Technology can be taught across a number of subjects.

Differentiated curricula and tiered assessment arrangements exist in some subjects and short courses are available in Technology, Information Technology, Modern European Languages and Welsh Second Language.

The GCSE is the main means of assessment at key stage 4.

Following the **Education Act 2002** which drew on the White Paper, *Schools Achieving Success*, more flexibility will be introduced into the Key Stage 4 curriculum, including the wider availability of vocational courses.

What can I do if I do not agree with the GCSE grades?

Strictly speaking it is the pupil, not the teacher, who can appeal to a board against a particular GCSE grading.

Teachers, however, do suggest to pupils that they may have a case. A teacher, through the Head, can always write to the board making valid points about the papers and marking.

An independent appeals authority has been set up to hear appeals from individuals and schools about the fitness of an examination board's appeal procedure and whether it was properly and fairly applied.

How much coursework is there nowadays?

Coursework at GCSE is undertaken under conditions prescribed by the board, approved by the Qualifications and Curriculum Authority (QCA). The work is marked by the teacher according to the board's criteria and will be externally moderated.

The percentage of coursework allowed varies from subject to subject but lies between 20% and 30% except for Technology which can be allowed as much as 60%.

Correct spelling and grammar

Marks are awarded in each GCSE subject for correct spelling, punctuation and grammar.

Other Courses

Schools may, and do, run courses outside the National Curriculum, and include examinations other than the GCSE. General National Vocational Qualifications are popular, and some schools have developed their own examination course, particularly in ICT.

Curriculum for 16–19 Year Olds

Advanced and Advanced Subsidiary levels

All post-16 students taking the Advanced Level GCE route can now take the Advanced Subsidiary (AS) courses in the first year of an A level course, or as a stand-alone examination. The A-level examination is now referred to as A2. It will be usual for A Level candidates to take at least four AS subjects which would be examined at the end of Year 12 and continue with three subjects at A Level (A2) into Year 13. More able students will also be able to take "world class tests" which will replace the old S Level and will be based on the A Level specification.

In addition all post-16 students are expected to develop "key skills" during their post 16 education. These "key skills" are:

- application of number
- communication
- information technology
- working with others
- improving own learning and performance
- problem solving.

All 16–plus students are expected to take a qualification in key skills alongside their main courses. The qualification is designed to meet the needs of employers who require these skills, and to make young people more employable.

All the A Level syllabuses have been re-written and are in a six-module format. The first three modules are at AS Level.

It will be possible for students to be flexible about when they sit the module assessments, either in January or July each year. Each module will be separately certificated.

The award will be graded from A–E.

Vocational courses: General National Vocational Qualifications (GNVQ)
There are three levels of GNVQ:

- foundation (usually taken in Years 10 and 11)
- intermediate
- and advanced.

More and more post-16 students are taking GNVQs at Intermediate or Advanced Level. Courses are available in Art and Design, Business, Health and Care, Leisure and Tourism, Manufacturing, Performing Arts. The full GNVQ comprises 12 modules, but it is possible for students to achieve a single award advanced GNVQ comprising six modules. A three-module award equivalent to the AS may be available in some subjects. GNVQs are administered by a number of bodies.

Literacy And Numeracy

Literacy and numeracy are two of the main strands of the Government's strategy to improve pupil achievement. The literacy strategy got underway in primary schools in 1998–1999 and the numeracy strategy in 1999–2000. Each governing body is required to nominate a "literacy" and a "numeracy" governor.

From September 2002 the key stage 3 National Strategy for Literacy will be introduced.

The Government guidance describes a "literate" pupil as one who:
- can read and write with confidence
- is a reasonable speller
- can write legibly
- knows a range of fiction and non-fiction
- is able to plan his or her work and edit it
- uses suitable vocabulary
- develops powers of imagination through an interest in books.

Literacy is not the preserve of English teachers. All teachers have a duty to improve pupils' literacy. The new National Curriculumn Orders all have a section focusing on the use of language.

Most secondary schools will now have policies for continuing the literacy focus established in primary schools.

The Government's teaching objectives from reception to Year 6 are set out in a folder, *The National Literacy Strategy: Framework for Teaching*. Although this guidance is not statutory, it is designed to help teachers to achieve a high standard of literacy in their pupils.

There are three strands which run through from reception to year 6:
- word level
- sentence level
- text level.

There are objectives for each term and the guidance recommends that 75% of the term's reading and writing should be within the designated range, with the other 25% being determined by Heads and teachers.

The third and fourth sections of the framework provides teachers with templates for planning purposes, plus technical advice.

The literacy hour

The literacy hour is not a statutory requirement, but the Government believes that it is a structure which provides a clear focus on literacy instruction. The framework advice is that the hour should be split into four periods:
- approximately 15 minutes shared reading and writing within the whole class
- approximately 15 minutes word level work
- approximately 20 minutes guided group work and individual work
- approximately 10 minutes of plenary work with the whole class to pull all the work together.

Heads and teachers have to decide how to achieve both a balance of activities and the coverage of the objectives over a term or half term.

It is likely that schools will have a weekly session to plan the process.

The numeracy hour

The numeracy hour should be split into three periods:

- approximately 10–15 minutes oral work and mental maths
- approximately 30–35 minutes for the main teaching activity, including numbers, calculations, shapes and measures and solving problems
- approximately 10–15 minutes for the whole class to review the work they have done.

Setting Targets

Schools have to set targets for pupil attainment at key stage 2 and the last year of compulsory schooling. The outcomes will be measured through National Curriculum tests, public examinations and equivalent qualifications.

Targets are statutorily required as follows:

- the percentage of pupils reaching level 4 or above in English and Mathematics at key stage 2
- the percentage of pupils getting five or more GCSEs or equivalent grades A*–C
- the percentage of pupils getting one or more GCSEs or equivalent grades A*–G.

If they wish, schools can add more targets of their own.

The first targets were set in Autumn 1998. From September 2000, schools have had to publish their actual achievement against those targets.

Targets for the new cohorts of pupils will be set each Autumn.

LEAs must include LEA targets, agreed with the DfES, in their Education Development Plans (EDPs) and must agree realistic targets with each of their schools.

Each school's performance will be reported each year in the School and College Performance Tables.

Heads of subject and each teacher of the subjects for which the school will be setting targets will need to collect and collate information about each pupil and each teaching group in order to make realistic predictions about their future performance in two years' time.

This target-setting will play a part in the new staff performance appraisal scheme.

Performance Targets

The **Education Act 1997** gave the Secretary of State power to require all maintained schools to set annual targets in respect of pupil performance. For pupils of compulsory school age, these would be National Curriculum assessments or public examination results. For other pupils, the targets would be public examinations or other external qualifications. The Government has set national targets for achievement at key stages and ocassionally revises the targets.

By 2004, 75% of 14 year olds should achieve level 5 in English, Maths and ICT and 70% in Science. By 2007, 85% of 14 years olds should achieve level 5 in English, Maths and ICT and 80% in Science.

Baseline Assessment

Each maintained primary school is required to adopt a baseline assessment scheme, which will apply to all children on entry to primary school. Heads will recommend to the governors a particular scheme chosen from a list accredited by the QCA. Where the school is maintained by the LEA, the Head and governors must first consider the LEA's own scheme.

Performance and Assessment Reports

Performance and Assessment Reports (PANDAs) are comprehensive sets of data on a school's performance, drawing on inspection evidence, test and examination results and teacher assessment. They are set out in the context of a school's socio-economic environment. They help schools understand how they are performing not only against national standards but also in comparison with other schools with similar characteristics.

Pupil Learning Credits

The Government has launched an initiative to boost access to activities such as computer classes, educational visits and music lessons for disadvantaged pupils. Initially it will benefit mainly key stage 3 pupils in certain areas

SPECIAL EDUCATIONAL NEEDS

Ever since the **Education Act 1981**, the needs of pupils with special educational needs have been given greater prominence. The expense and complexities of the requirements led to much dissatisfaction and considerable overhaul was made in 1993.

A child has special educational needs if he or she has a learning difficulty which calls for a special educational provision.

Each school has a duty to identify such difficulties and to make proper provision for the variety of needs.

The **Special Educational Needs and Disability Act 2001** has strengthened the right of parents to mainstream schooling for their children. Each LEA will have "independent parental supporters" to ensure that parents of children with SEN get advice and information. A new Special Educational Needs Code of Practice was issued in November 2001.

If appropriate, the LEA will make a statement of special educational needs setting out what the problem is and the provision to be made. The LEA will also monitor and review the provision.

Each school should have a detailed special educational needs policy agreed by the governing body and a report has to be made annually to the parents.

All teachers have a duty to take account of the policy in their teaching and dealing with children who are deemed to have special educational needs.

Individual Education Plans

Individual Education Plans (IEPs) are part of the Government's social inclusion policy. Schools are expected to identify pupils with problems for whom an IEP should be drawn up. An IEP will usually focus on three targets at most and will involve parents and pupils as well as teachers and others (eg educational psychologist, or care workers).

Disability

Part II of the **Special Needs and Disability Act 2001** places responsibility on LEAs and schools not to treat pupils with disabilities less favourably than other pupils without justification and to make reasonable adjustments so as not to put disabled students at substantial disadvantage.

CURRICULUM ISSUES

Discrimination Against Pupils

Schools should not discriminate against pupils or employees. Even single sex schools should do their best to provide a full range of subjects that ought to be available to both boys and girls.

Schools cannot deny a pupil access to a particular sport solely on the grounds of sex — although safety considerations may need to be taken into account.

It is also likely to be discriminatory to prevent a girl from wearing trousers in school. It would be up to the school to prove that this was not a discriminatory prohibition.

Political Education

Politics can appear in the school curriculum as a subject or can be part of other subjects.

The treatment of controversial political issues in schools is covered by ss.44 and 45 of the **Education (No.2) Act 1986** (now consolidated in the **Education Act 1996**). Further guidance is provided in Circular 7/87 *Education (No.2) Act 1986: Further Guidance (Annex 11).*

LEAs, governing bodies and Heads have to forbid:

- the pursuit of partisan political activities by any of the junior pupils registered at the school
- the promotion of partisan political views in the teaching of any subject in the school.

When the political activities take place off-site, the first point above applies only where arrangements are made for junior pupils to take part in activities arranged by a member of staff of the school (in his or her capacity as such).

Schools also have to ensure, as far as is reasonably practicable, that where political issues are introduced in the school they are in a balanced presentation of opposing views.

LEAs, governing bodies and Heads have to make judgments about what contributes a "balanced presentation of opposing views". It does not mean that all views must be represented.

The intention behind the sections is not to stifle political debate but to ensure that political indoctrination does not take place.

Schools may well have policies about the treatment of politically sensitive issues and teachers should adhere to such policies.

Circular 7/87 encourages teachers to tackle controversial political issues in accordance with the above principles. Teachers should distinguish between fact and fiction and be ready to acknowledge their own bias but should encourage pupils to form their own opinions. How this is best done is a matter for professional judgment.

Sex Education

The issue of sex education is covered in the **Education (No. 2) Act 1986** (now consolidated in the **Education Act 1996**). Guidance is provided in the Government's *Sex and Relationship Education Guidance,* reference DfES 0116/2000, to which schools must have a regard. The guidance states that the school has a responsibility to draw up a written policy for the provision of sex education. It must:

- define sex and relationship education
- describe how it should be provided and who is responsible for providing it
- explain how it is monitored and evaluated
- be reviewed regularly
- explain that parents have the right to withdraw their children from those parts of the curriculum that are not part of the National Curriculum.

A summary of the policy must be published in the school prospectus.

In maintained primary schools, governing bodies must consider at what stage, if at all, sex education should be introduced. They must keep an up-to-date written policy statement, available to parents.

Middle schools must make the appropriate arrangements according to whether they are deemed primary or secondary schools.

In maintained secondary schools, sex education (including education about AIDS and other sexually transmitted diseases) must be provided for all pupils. The secondary school policy must state how sex and relationship education contributes not only to the National Curriculum, but also to PSHE and citizenship education. Again policy statements must be available.

In all maintained schools, sex education must be provided in such a way as to encourage young people to have regard to moral considerations and the value of family life.

Can parents withdraw pupils from sex education?

Parents of any pupil at a maintained school can withdraw a pupil from all or part of the sex education. However, the biological aspects of human reproduction and changes in adolescence that are part of National Curriculum subjects remain compulsory for all pupils.

Teachers should be aware of the sensitive nature of the issues and school governors and senior management should ensure that teachers consider the best way of introducing and teaching the issues.

The legislation does not prevent an objective discussion of homosexuality and the counselling of pupils about their sexuality. However, homosexuality is not to be presented as the "norm" nor as a pretended family relationship.

Parents' Rights to Withdraw Pupils from Areas of the Curriculum

Parents have a right to withdraw their children from Religious Education and non-National Curriculum sex education. They do not have a right to withdraw from other areas of the curriculum unless the Head agrees — usually by exercising his or her right to temporarily exempt pupils from National Curriculum provisions in certain circumstances.

Personal, Social and Health Education

Personal, Social and Health Education (PSHE) now forms part of the non-statutory curriculum at key stages 1–4. The Government guidance includes work in lesson time and a wide range of other activities.

All schools should have a health education policy incorporated into their health and safety policy. It is likely to include details of alcohol, smoking and drugs education and increasingly a healthy eating policy and healthy lifestyle programme.

The study of health and safety issues forms part of each pupil's entitlement at each key stage.

Drugs and solvent abuse

All teachers should be aware of the school's policy on drug and solvent abuse. It is important for swift and appropriate action to be taken and, therefore, teachers must appreciate their role and use professional expertise and sensitivity when confronted by difficult situations.

Citizenship

Citizenship is now a statutory part of the secondary school curriculum. It is non-statutory but expected in primary schools.

The aim is to ensure that Citizenship gives pupils the knowledge, understanding and skills to enable them to participate in society as active citizens of our democracy.

The attainment target is "to become informed, active and responsible citizens".

Religious Education

Schools are required by the **Education Reform Act 1988** (now consolidated in the **Education Act 1996**) to ensure that the curriculum is balanced and broadly based and promotes the spiritual, moral, cultural, mental and physical development of pupils and prepares them for adult life.

The school curriculum for pupils up to year 13 must include Religious Education.

All county and voluntary controlled schools must provide Religious Education for all pupils in accordance with locally agreed syllabuses. These syllabuses must reflect the fact that the religious traditions in the UK are in the main Christian, while taking into account the practices of other principal religions represented in the UK. Christian religious education should be non-denominational.

In aided and special agreement schools, the governors determine the syllabus in accordance with any trust deed.

If a parent requires Religious Education that is different from that provided by the school, it may be arranged on or off the premises.

There are no nationally prescribed programmes of study or attainment targets or national assessment arrangements, although Religious Education can be taken as a subject at GCSE and/or A level.

Do I as a teacher have to take part in Religious Education teaching?

Neither Heads nor teachers are obliged to teach Religious Education, nor must they be discriminated against for holding particular religious views.

In controlled and special agreement schools, governors can appoint "reserved teachers" to teach particular religious instruction.

In aided schools, all teachers should be appointed for their fitness to teach Religious Education in the particular way required by the school. Teachers applying to such schools should be aware of the requirements.

Collective Worship

By virtue of s.6 of the **Education Reform Act 1988** (now consolidated in the **School Standards and Framework Act 1998**), all pupils must take part in a daily act of worship. The law does not require the pupils to come together in the same place at the same time. The worship can be in houses or year groups or class groups.

The worship must be "wholly or mainly of a broadly Christian character but not distinctive of a particular Christian denomination". A collective act is not necessarily corporate. It implies, therefore, a freedom for individuals to worship individually even though gathered in a body.

Can parents withdraw their children from collective worship?

Parents have a right, under the **Education Act 1996**, to withdraw their children from collective worship.

Do teachers have to join in collective worship?

Neither Heads nor teachers in county schools are obliged to take part in collective worship, although Heads must make arrangements for it to take place. Teachers are, however, obliged to attend the non-religious parts of assembly if directed to do so (*School Teachers' Pay and Conditions Document*).

Can material other than Christian material be included?

Circular 1/94 *Religious Education and Collective Worship* points out that the majority of acts of worship in a school year must be of a broadly Christian character, but material from other sources can be included.

Careers Education

The **Education Act 1997** states all publicly funded schools must provide a programme of careers education in years 9–11. They must also provide access to careers advisors and work with careers services to ensure that pupils have access to careers guidance materials. It is recommended in Circular 5/97 *Careers Education and Guidance in Schools* that an agreement is reached with the Careers Service on how best to fulfil these obligations.

ADMINISTRATIVE REQUIREMENTS

Class Sizes

The Secretary of State is empowered to impose limits on class sizes during ordinary teaching lessons by a single qualified teacher.

Infant classes are now restricted to an upper limit of 30 pupils.

Apart from that, it is a matter for the Head to determine in the light of the general ratio of staff to pupils.

Health and safety factors must be taken into account in determining maximum numbers in any one area.

A teacher has a duty to bring to the Head's attention any concern over safety aspects. A teacher who does this is protected by the **Employment Rights Act 1996** against dismissal or action short of dismissal.

Curriculum Records

A curricular record has to be kept for each pupil at maintained schools (**Pupil Information Regulations 2000**). The Regulations are explained in Circular 0015/2000. A curricular record is defined as a formal record of a pupil's academic achievements, his or her other skills and abilities and the progress he or she has made at the school.

Teaching Methods

Teachers have a duty to liaise and co-operate with the Head and colleagues on the preparation and development of courses of study, materials, programmes, methods of teaching and assessment and pastoral arrangements.

The National Curriculum legislation specifically forbids any Government orders requiring particular methods of providing subjects on a school timetable or specifying particular teaching methods, books or materials. These are matters for professional decisions by the subject department and individual teachers.

How much homework should I set?

There are no statutory requirements, but following a critical Ofsted report in 1995 and subsequent research, the Government issued non-statutory guidelines in 1998. The recommended time allocation for homework is as follows.

Primary schools

Years 1 and 2, 1 hour per week (reading, spelling, other literacy and number work).

Years 3 and 4, 1 hour per week (literacy, numeracy with occasional assignments in other subjects).

Years 5 and 6, 30 mins per day (regular weekly schedule with emphasis on literacy and numeracy but also a wider range of subjects).

Secondary schools

Years 7 and 8, 45-90 mins per day.

Year 9, 1–2 hours per day.

Years 10 and 11, 1–2 hours per day.

Years 12 and 13, depends on each individual subject programme, but guidance should be included in school policies.

Public Examinations

The traditional examination boards have now formed themselves into large groupings, mainly for marketing purposes. It is possible for schools to use syllabuses from more than one board. This will be a matter for the school to decide.

Teachers are obliged to participate in arrangements for preparing pupils for public examinations and in assessing pupils for the purposes of such examinations, to record and report such assessments and to participate in pupils presentation for and supervision during such examinations.

Teachers are required to carry out duties under the reasonable direction of the Head. What individual teachers teach will be set out in department/subject programmes of study. These programmes of study must reflect the requirements of the National Curriculum for pupils of compulsory school age, but can include other matters too. The methods of teaching to be used are not specified in legislation and will be matters for the subject department and individual teachers to determine as part of their professionalism.

Performance Tables

Each year governing bodies have to provide the DfES with information about examination results, attendance and other issues for the preparation of national analyses. Schools' performances are published in tables annually.

Copyright

Modern reprographic and recording facilities make copying very easy. It would be marvellous to be able to copy bits of this and that as necessary but in all probability the original source will be covered by copyright.

This means that someone has the legal right to decide whether a piece of writing, or film or music, or computer software can be copied or reproduced by someone else.

Copyright legislation gives protection to authors and to other owners of the copyright. Protection can last for up to 50 years. The **Copyright, Design and Patents Act 1988** also provides for reasonable access to be made to those who wish to copy for learning purposes.

What items are protected?

Literary works, computer programmes, dramatic and musical and artistic works, sound recordings, films, videos and cable programmes are among the works covered.

Each one of these types is protected in its own right, so a photograph of a painting contains two distinct copyright elements.

Although generally no one may copy copyright material without the permission of the owner, education users can benefit from exceptions which allow them to copy without permission.

The concessionary areas are described in an information sheet *Copyright — The Act of 1988* issued by the British Educational Communications and Technology Agency (BECTA). The Agency publishes other guides too.

Further information is obtainable from the Rights Development Office, BCETA, 3 Devonshire Street, London W1N 2BA. Schools should inform members of staff of the rules for copying.

Copyright licensing
A scheme for licensed copying of books, periodicals and journals in schools is organised through the Copyright Licensing Agency. Each maintained school should have a copy of the agreement and instructions as to how it operates. The licence does not currently cover independent schools.

Similar schemes for off-air recording and copying sound recordings are also in existence.

The Educational Copyright Users' Forum provides advice and monitors licensing arrangements.

Licences

Governing bodies control the use of school premises in general, but for some activities a licence will be required.

In certain circumstances a licence will be required for a musical entertainment held outdoors if the local district council requires it. Public entertainments indoors such as music, dancing or sports of a martial nature need a licence, but sales of work, debates, quiz shows or meetings do not attract licensing.

The Home Office takes the view that such entertainments promoted by a school's Parent–Teacher Organisation, attended only by pupils, parents and their guests, would not constitute public entertainment.

Licences are also required if a school wishes to sell alcohol at a school event, or at an event in the school run by an outside body.

Licences may also be required if a school wishes to hold a raffle or lottery. It is important to know what the local authority's regulations are.

Examinations: Data Protection

Personal data recorded by a candidate in an examination is exempt from subject access rules. In the case of examination marks the period in which access must be granted is five months from the date of the request or 40 days from the announcement of the results, whichever is the shorter.

Can I put on class plays for the rest of the year group without obtaining permission?

Public performances of plays on school premises (whether school plays or plays performed in school by others) require a licence under the **Theatre Act 1968**. However, it is not thought likely that plays performed before only parents, teachers, pupils, families and guests would constitute a "public performance", and, therefore, no licence is necessary.

Schools must also apply for, and pay for, permission to perform a play which is still under copyright. Even a 400 year old Shakespeare play will require permission to be performed if the edition being used is itself under copyright.

There is no requirement to obtain a licence if you are simply performing a play for educational purposes to pupils in the school.

INDEX

A

B

D

E

J

L

M

N

O

P

Q

R

S

T

U

V

W

Order Form — Teachers' Rights, Duties and Responsibilities

Please fill in this form if you would like to order further copies of Teachers' Rights, Duties and Responsibilities

1. Details of order

I would like to order ______ copies of Croner's Teachers' Rights, Duties and Responsibilities @ £17.50 per copy (£16 per copy plus £1.50 ppa).

Discounts: buy 10+ and receive a 5% discount, 20+ and receive a 10% discount, 30+ and receive a 20% discount.

Books will be despatched with an invoice.

2. Order details — please complete

Name:

Job title:

Company:

Address:

Postcode:

Telephone number: **Date:**

3. Your signature:______________________________

4. Further information

If you would like to order other books from Croner.CCH, please tick:

❑ School Governor's Legal Guide, £30 (including ppa). Bound book, 200 pages.
❑ School Sports and the Law, £16 (including ppa). Bound Book, 126 pages.

5. How to order

- Telephone Customers Services on 020 8247 1261, or
- Fill in your details, fold in half, seal outside edges and post this reply paid device.

VDHVC

BUSINESS REPLY SERVICE
Licence No KT1332

Alex Herrington
Croner.CCH Group Limited
145 London Road
Kingston upon Thames
Surrey
KT2 6BR